THE GAY MAN'S
GUIDE
TO GROWING
OLDER

THE GAY MAN'S GUIDE TO GROWING OLDER

JOHN LOCKHART

alyson books
los angeles | new york

MANUFACTURED IN THE UNITED STATES OF AMERICA.

THIS TRADE PAPERBACK ORIGINAL IS PUBLISHED BY ALYSON PUBLICATIONS,
P.O. BOX 4371, LOS ANGELES, CALIFORNIA 90078-4371.
DISTRIBUTION IN THE UNITED KINGDOM BY TURNAROUND PUBLISHER SERVICES LTD.,
UNIT 3, OLYMPIA TRADING ESTATE, COBURG ROAD, WOOD GREEN,
LONDON N22 6TZ ENGLAND.

FIRST EDITION: JUNE 2002

02 03 04 05 06 ▓ 10 9 8 7 6 5 4 3 2 1

ISBN 1-55583-591-0

CREDITS
COVER DESIGN BY LOUIS MANDRAPILIAS.
FRONT COVER PHOTOGRAPH BY JOHN SKALICKY.
BACK COVER PHOTOGRAPH BY CAROL PIERCE.

This book is dedicated to
Robert Alston Ricks
1915-1998
World War II hero, mentor, true friend,
world's best travel companion, Southern gentleman

CONTENTS

ACKNOWLEDGMENTS

I would like to thank:

Bob, 82, who lives in Arizona and triggered the idea for this book. When I visited him—we hadn't seen each other for nearly 20 years—I thought I would like to know, at age 67, what to expect if I should live to be Bob's age. From our informal weekend discussion, the concept for *The Gay Man's Guide to Growing Older* emerged.

Bruce Kerschner, owner of the Obelisk Bookstore in San Diego, for support and encouragement and for introducing me to Scott Brassart, editor in chief and associate publisher at Alyson Publications.

Dr. Cecil J. Hannan, Senator Lucy Killea, and Dr. Carol Pierce for being my first sounding boards, for their focusing questions and comments, for their content contributions, for listening to me through the interview and writing process, for their suggestions, for helping to shape the book, and for their friendship.

Amy Dean, Adrienne Danzig, Molly Hannan, Mark Hunter, Fentress Ott, and Rick Pyles for their counsel, for listening, for suggesting, and for their friendship and support, and for always asking, "How is the book going?"

The wonderful people who helped connect me to the men of *The Gay Man's Guide to Growing Older:* Dave Allen, my longtime friend and travel consultant; Ellen Ensig-Brodsky; Pride Senior Network; Peter Lundberg; Our Town; Sandy Warshaw; Senior Action in A Gay Environment (SAGE); my friends Mel Merrill Nicole Murray-Ramirez, Steve Nottle, Chris Rogers, Larry Sorensen, and J. W. White.

The cadre of computer geniuses, without whom *The Gay Man's Guide to Growing Older* would not have happened: Gary Paul, for transcribing hours of interview tapes, creating databases, for invaluable and always patient computer instruction, and for responding to every comment or editorial question with "That's your decision"; Dan Valins, for organizing the entire book on the computer—I still don't know how he did it—and for integrating interview text into chapter format and mentoring me through the mysteries of writing on a computer; and Miles Durfee, for responding to my sometimes frantic calls for help.

The 41 men who made *The Gay Man's Guide to Growing Older* possible. Thank you for your candor and openness, for sharing your lives, for demonstrating that life is good, worthwhile, and positive. You are heroes to me and to generations of gay men to come.

And Scott Brassart, Alyson Publications editor in chief, for his upbeat approach, his sure head and hand that always improved the content while honing the point, for eliminating duplications, and yes, for telling me to make cuts of material that was "just not that interesting."

INTRODUCTION

Despite its universality, aging remains one of the least discussed, least studied, and, probably as a result, least celebrated aspects of gay and lesbian lives."
—*Completely Queer: The Gay and Lesbian Encyclopedia,*
by Steve Hogan and Lee Hudson

The Gay Man's Guide to Growing Older is a practical, nonacademic book about what life is like for gay men over 65, based on the experiences of those who are already there. In-depth one-on-one interviews with 41 men from a variety of economic, educational, cultural, racial, and ethnic backgrounds form the backbone of the text. In one instance, two men, partners Fred and Clee of San Francisco, participated jointly in the discussion. In several other cases, the interviewee's partner participated somewhat or sat in on the conversation. A comprehensive questionnaire guided the 41 men interviewed through issues relating to money, health, self-image, retirement, living options, spirituality, relationships, sex, and more. For a brief biography of each man interviewed, please see "Pride of Place" following this introduction.

Life expectancy in the United States has increased since 1900 from 47 to just under 83. The largest single population group in the country now consists of people over 65—approximately 20%. A study by the AARP reports that "quality, not quantity in later years" is the priority for most older individuals. Declining health leads as a primary concern for older Americans, with 46% of the AARP study respondents rating it a top issue; followed by lack of money, 38%; and fear of losing mental facilities, 13%. Only 8% worry about living in a nursing home. AARP also reports that people between the ages of 18 and 24 want to live to age 83. Those over 75, however, say they want to live to age 96.

The 41 men interviewed range in age from 65 to 91. Their average age at the time of interview was 72 years, 10 months. The men are now living in 13 states and the District of Columbia. Just as important as where they live now is where they grew up and lived the bulk of their lives. Like many older Americans, gay men gravitate to the Sun Belt for their retirement years, and this book's interviewees are no exception. Nearly to a man, they grew up, worked, and lived most of their lives outside the Sun Belt.

The following statistics, though not scientific, are garnered from information provided in the interviews. All summary results and conclusions are based on information given at the time of the interviews.

Most of the men interviewed knew they were gay by their early teens—but one man was sure he was gay at age 2, and six didn't realize it until reaching their 20s. The average age for knowing they were gay is 10 years, 3 months.

When asked about their political beliefs, 52% self-identify as liberals, 44% as middle-of-the-road, 1% as conservative, and 1% as independent. Fifty percent of the men consider themselves politically active. With just two exceptions—one a resident alien, the other a man who had lived abroad for many years and had not registered to vote upon returning to the United States—all of the men vote regularly.

Eighty-three percent of the men are retired, but nearly half of the retirees, 37% overall, work full- or part-time jobs. More than half of the men, 55%, perform volunteer work, often at AIDS service agencies. Others volunteer in community efforts or in connection with their previous careers.

Ninety percent believe the money they have will last for their lifetime. Thirty of the men receive Social Security, 24 receive retirement income, 25 have investment income, and 18 receive income from other sources. Nineteen percent of the men interviewed have a total annual income of $19,999 or less; 24% have an income of $20,000–$29,999; 19% have an income of $30,000–$39,999; 8% have an income of $40,000–$49,999; 3% have an income of $50,000–$59,999; 8% have an income of $60,000–$69,999; and 19% have an income over $70,000. (One man declined to state his total annual income.) Eighty-three percent of the men are not financially responsible for others in any way. Eight percent report that they help others financially. Thirty-eight men have a will, 24 have a living trust, and some have both.

On average the men spend 1.9 hours a day watching television. Eighty percent of the men view newscasts, 85% read the newspaper daily, 49% own a computer, and 56% use E-mail regularly. If they do not own a computer, they access their E-mail by using computers at the public library or borrowing friends' computers. Forty-nine percent surf the World Wide Web as well.

Forty-eight percent of the men describe their health as "excellent," 10% as "very good," 33% as "good," 7% as "fair," and 3% as "poor." A number of the men have surgical histories, mainly related to heart and prostate conditions. None of the men report that they are HIV-positive, though several have lost partners to AIDS-related illnesses. Ninety-five percent of the men do not smoke, but 76% once did. Sixty-five percent drink alcohol, and 21% report that alcohol has been a problem for them. Almost without exception, the men have no experience with recreational drug use—one man even asked, "What are recreational drugs?" Just one man regularly uses hard drugs. Nearly all the men have basic health care through HMOs or other arrangements, and 27% have purchased a long-term health care program. Power of attorney for health care access is a high priority: 79% of the men have it.

Eighty percent of the men own their living space. Fifteen men live in houses, 14 in apartments or condominiums, and the rest live in other types of housing, such as manufactured homes and lifetime-care communities. Twenty of the men live alone, 14 live with partners, and the remainder live with friends or roommates. A large majority of the men interviewed, 83%, plan to stay where they are. Eighty percent of the men own a car; 85% are licensed to drive. Two of the men have never learned to drive.

Forty-nine percent of the men have been married; three have been married twice. One of the men reports that he "may still be married." Forty-four percent of the men are currently in a romantic relationship with another man. Fifty-four percent claim gay marriage isn't a high priority for them, though 83% advocate extending domestic-partner benefits to same-sex couples. For 70% of the men, sex is important. Twenty-one percent state they have used Viagra.

Fifty-five percent of the men served in the military. Several were kicked out for being gay or were refused entry because they acknowledged their homosexuality at the time of induction. Two men served in foreign military forces before coming to the United States.

Eighty-four percent of the men believe in a supreme being, but only 47% believe there is an afterlife. Eighteen percent said they are unsure if there is an afterlife. Forty-nine percent belong to an established religion. Of those adhering to established religious beliefs, only 30% are regular communicants. Only 21% view religious affiliation as important. Ninety percent, however, assert that ethical principles drive their life.

PRIDE OF PLACE

Robert of Palm Desert, 91, is the oldest man interviewed for this book. He grew up in Grand Rapids, Mich., served in World War II, and after a long, full career retired to the Southern California desert, where he swims daily. He sings and dances for fun. Still very active, Robert had to postpone his interview for this book because he flew to France on a spur-of-the moment trip.

Clee, 83, and his partner, **Fred**, 77, make their home in San Francisco. They met in Los Angeles in 1953 and moved together to San Francisco a few years later—into the house they still live in today. Pillars of the neighborhood, they go on daily strolls together and still enjoy a closeness apparent to anyone they meet.

Ed of Oakland, 83, a retired San Francisco social worker, and his partner, Bob, 80, live high above Lake Merritt and downtown Oakland in a sunny two-bedroom apartment in St. Paul's Towers, a lifetime-care community operated by the Episcopal Foundation. Together for 55 years, Ed and Bob found the environment at St. Paul's Towers welcoming when they moved in as an openly gay couple 16 years ago. Now, they are still glad they made that decision. As far as they know, they are the sole openly gay or lesbian couple residing at St. Paul's Towers.

Bob, 82, of Arizona retired to a life of skiing and hiking after a career as a civilian Pentagon employee during and after World War II. Bob has led cross-country hikes in the United States and United Kingdom. He designed and helped cut and lay a 3.5-mile trail in a municipal desert park. Today, Bob keeps an eye on that trail to monitor its use and maintenance.

Mike, 79, lives in a Southern California beach community. His roots, though, are in South Boston. To this day he retains a unique Boston mindset as well as that city's accent. Mike enlisted in the Navy during World War II, served as a Seabee, and retired after 20 years service. Formerly married and the father of three, he walks most every day year-round from his apartment near the Pacific to a special beach spot amid low sand dunes—a round-trip of nearly 10 miles.

Robert Tingling, 79, of Coral Sands, Fla., emigrated to the United States from Jamaica, where he had lived for 38 years. He attended college in the Midwest and lived in several cities before moving to South Florida at the behest of his sister. Robert is proud of his diverse ethnic heritage—English, Welsh, Chinese, East Indian, African—and feels he has benefited tremendously by living in numerous cultures and environments.

José Sarría, 78, of Lake County, Calif., was the first openly gay man to run for public office in the United States: San Francisco City and County Supervisor in 1961. José enjoyed a legendary long run at the city's Black Cat Cabaret, where he performed in drag as an impressionist and comic with a special penchant for lampooning opera. A tiger for causes he believes in, José relates strongly to his Latino heritage. He is planning to move from rural Lake County to Palm Springs.

Richard Malloy, 78, and his partner, Tucker, 77, are in the arts: Richard is a stage and television actor, and Tucker is a painter. In their 54 years together, they have lived "all over the world" but now reside in Springfield, Va., a suburb of Washington, D.C. Richard says the one constant over the course of their long relationship has been caring for their beloved dogs.

Ben Fowler, 77, of San Diego was a married career U.S. Army officer for a number of years. He also moonlighted as a model for art classes and various publications. Today, Ben is a leather daddy with his own Web site, Daddy Ben's. He met his partner, Lee, or "Boy" as Ben sometimes calls him, on the Internet. They share a town house near the beach in a neighborhood where Ben has lived since 1980.

Virgil Hylton, 77, lives in a condominium in Fort Myers, Fla., where he enjoys the Gulf Coast climate and his part-time job. He grew up as one of five children on a farm near Willis, Va. The post–World War II GI bill was his ticket out of rural Virginia to higher education and a career as a chemical engineer. Once married but now divorced from his wife, he is the father of two daughters and a son who died as a teenager.

John Peters, 75, of Eldridge, Iowa, was married to a woman who died 11 years into their marriage, leaving him to raise their 9-year-old son as a single parent. John's life is centered in Eldridge, a small town of fewer than 4,000 residents, as well as in the nearby

Quad Cities area, a cluster of small industrial cities along the Mississippi River border of Iowa and Illinois. A dedicated community volunteer, he is a member of the Older Iowa Legislature, where each year he attends sessions and chairs legislative committees.

Tom Pait, 75, of San Francisco is a hearty physical man well-known in running circles as a master marathoner. A runner since 1980, Tom has completed more than 60 marathons and participated in countless 5-kilometer and 10-kilometer races and half marathons. A stalwart of Front Runners San Francisco, Tom enjoys living in the center of the city without an automobile.

Charles, 73, commutes from his large turn-of-the-century house in New Jersey to his Wall Street job, where he handles his company's client investment records. He enjoys his job but finds that his Saturdays are filled with the tasks of running a household. Charles's 42-year relationship ended with his partner's death in 1998. A lifetime East Coaster, Charles grew up in New York City and Hartford, Conn.

Bud Jordan, 73, of Palm Springs traces his roots to Cincinnati and a farm in Kentucky. He migrated west and lived in the Los Angeles area with his partner, Vic, whose death in 1994 ended their 42-year relationship. Bud now lives in the Southern California desert and shares a home with his close friend, Norman Eckelberger, who in turn shares his life with Steve Scott in nearby Palm Desert.Steve and Norman were also interviewed for this book.

Frank Poe, 73, of Palm Springs lives with his beloved dog in a condominium in a quiet garden-like setting. His is originally from Tennessee, where his father was state commissioner for conservation. After living briefly in Delaware near his twin brother, Frank came to California when he was 30. His life with his partner, Ed Wright, spanned more than 20 years and was his sole long-term gay relationship. It ended several years ago with Ed's death at age 81.

Robert Bettinger, 72, of Cardiff-by-the-Sea, Calif., and his partner, Charles, live and work at the San Elijo Lagoon Reserve, an 885-acre salt marsh lagoon that is one of the few remaining wetlands on California's coast. His is an ordained Episcopal priest. Formerly married, he is the father of four daughters and grandfather of three.

Ed Conlon, 72, of San Diego was born on a river barge in the Hudson River, where he lived until age 6 with the New York City skyline and the Statue of Liberty as a backdrop. As a young man he served in the Navy and later lived in Erie, Pa. For the last 25 years, he has called San Diego home and has been known to don drag and transform into Queen Eddie, a fixture in the city's Pride parade. A cancer survivor, Ed views his 41-year relationship with his partner, Shawne, as the one constant in his life. Ed writes a social and advice column for a San Diego gay and lesbian community newspaper.

Jon Borset, 71, of San Francisco grew up in Detroit and is an avid sportsman, like his friend Tom Pait. Jon's sport is race-walking, and his first race-walking marathon was in 1991. He has completed 30 since then. An Alpine skiing enthusiast, Jon divides his time between his getaway in the Sierra Nevada Mountains and the predominantly Asian-American San Francisco neighborhood he has called home for over 30 years.

John Kiley, 71, of New York City is a native of Adelaide, South Australia. A naturalized American citizen, he grew up both in the center of Australia and on the coast. John plans to sell the meetings-and-motivation business he has owned for many years, but he hopes to retain some interest in its daily operation so that he can maintain professional contacts. John had been in the United States for only 18 months in the early 1950s when he met his partner Gene, now 71. They have since split their time between their apartment in Manhattan and trips to Australia. As avid runners and swimmers, John and Gene look forward to Gay Games VI, which will be held in Sydney in November 2002.

John Schiappi, 71, of Washington, D.C., enjoyed a 40-year career at the Bureau of National Affairs, a publisher of news and reference materials focusing on legal and regulatory developments affecting both business and the public sector. John's area of expertise was labor relations. He began as an editor and had risen to vice president for human resources by the time he retired in 1994. John served on the BNA board of directors for more than 15 years and currently is a 10-year board member of the Whitman-Walker Clinic, the capital's primary clinic serving PWAs and the gay and lesbian community. Married for 20 years, John never divorced his wife; she is now deceased. He is the father of two.

George Casper, 70, of Boston has been a cover boy for a quarterly magazine for mature men and their admirers. He grew up on a farm in Ohio and had a career as an engineer in California and Massachusetts. He has two children and was married for 23 years before divorcing his wife. Nowadays, George works part-time in his sister's travel agency and enthusiastically participates in Boston's "favorite indoor sport: politics." George is a veteran of several gay male relationships, many of which have been inter-generational.

Milton Lestz, 70, of Fort Lauderdale grew up on New York City's Lower East Side. For many years he owned and operated an antique business in New Jersey. Milton shared his home and life with his partner of 35 years, who died of cancer in 1996. After moving to South Florida, he jumped into gay and lesbian commu-nity issues and established a gay men's discussion group in which he regularly participates. He swims daily.

Steve Scott, 70, of Palm Desert is one-eighth Cherokee. The youngest of 13 children, he grew up in a Mormon family in Utah and lived on a farm until he was 12. Art school in Mexico led to a career as a fashion designer in New York City. He then owned a Los Angeles real estate brokerage firm, which he sold when he was 53 to concentrate on writing. Steve has recently published a mystery novel, *Echo Park,* and moved to the Southern California desert.

Jim Edmonds, 69, of Cheney, Wash., grew up in an all-white neighborhood in Pittsfield, Mass. Similarly, today, Jim and his three older sisters constitute one of the few African-American households in their community, a small college town in eastern Washington state. Jim has enjoyed a distinguished career in music: a professor-ship at Eastern Washington University, two music-study sabbati-cals in Europe, and tenure as president of the Washington State

Music Teachers Association. In 1985 he established the Northwest Woodwind Trio along with two other musicians. The trio has toured the United States and released a compact disc. They perform a repertoire spanning three centuries and have been featured on National Public Radio.

George of New York City, 69, is naturalized American citizen of French-Canadian origin. He grew up in Fall River, Mass., and now lives in a West Side co-op. He considers himself "semiretired" as an investment relations consultant. An avid walker, George loves to explore the city on foot, sometimes combining his walk with a visit to a gallery or museum.

Cyprian Fary, 68, of Thousand Palms, Calif., is a native of the part of Czechoslovakia that is now the Republic of Slovakia. Now a naturalized American citizen, Cyprian came to the United States at age 24 as a political refugee after a dramatic escape in Hamburg, West Germany, from behind the Iron Curtain: "When I got to Hamburg, I got my suitcase at 3 A.M. I left the boat. I didn't go back!" Cyprian grew up with three siblings on a farm and experienced the Nazi occupation of his village during World War II as well as the war's end, the Communist takeover of his country, and life under Communist rule. After a career as a chef with the U.S. Merchant Marine, Cyprian worked as a security person for former ambassador Walter H. Annenberg before retiring.

Mel Clark, 68, Annapolis, Md., grew up on a Missouri farm and then went off to college, eventually earning an advanced degree in electrical engineering. He was a general contractor for 19 years in New Mexico, where he built and remodeled residential and commercial buildings. In the mid 1980s, Mel moved to Maryland, where he obtained a contractor's license and has since owned and operated a construction business, which he hopes to turn over to somebody else soon. Mel and his partner have been together for 17 years, and he was in a heterosexual marriage for nearly the same length of time.

Ron Dropkin, 68, of New York City resides in a spacious high-floor Manhattan apartment he acquired many years ago. Light and airy, it overlooks a greensward with mature trees not far from Lincoln Center. A retired public school teacher, Ron shares his home with his partner of 15 years, a native of Japan who works full-time as a designer of men's clothing. Together, they enjoy their country house too. Ron sees himself as an existentialist and believes that good comes as the result of individual action.

Jim of Michigan, 67, is of black, white, and Native American ethnicity. He retired 20 years ago from a Big 3 automaker, where he worked in financial accounting. He was in a gay relationship for nearly 13 years and is a Korean War veteran.

Warde Laidman, 67, of Oakland originally hails from the Canadian province of Saskatchewan. He grew up in a prairie town of fewer than 500 inhabitants, where he started grammar school and graduated from high school with the same group of class-mates. Warde holds degrees from two Canadian universities. A naturalized American citizen, he spent his career as a mental health professional in San Francisco. Warde has never been in a hetero-sexual marriage. He and his partner for 38 years, Hadley Dale Hall, met at work. Both men retired in 1987.

Jim Mitchell, 67, of Lake Peekskill, N.Y., earned a graduate degree from England's Oxford University and has since pursued further advanced study. He was a career social studies teacher in the New York City public schools and the openly gay president of his 1,100-member union before retiring from that position. Although he has never been married to a woman, Jim is a veteran of four gay relationships and is also financially responsible for a 31-year-old male ward who lives in Appleton, Wis. Jim has been making frequent trips to Wisconsin but expects his ward to move to New York eventually. Though he faces the probability of blindness within 10 years due to macular degeneration, Jim nevertheless retains a positive outlook on the future.

Lee Denman, 66, of Oceanside, Calif., grew up in the Chicago suburbs but has lived all over the world—27 countries in all—while prospecting for oil as a petroleum engineer. Today, Lee is the treasurer of the Capri Lounge, his nephew's gay and lesbian bar in Oceanside, a Southern California beach community near the U.S. Marine Corps Base at Camp Pendleton. Though he's permanently settled in Oceanside, Lee feels his overseas life of constant travel has prevented him from developing close relationships.

Norman Eckelberger, 66, of Palm Springs considers himself a "Valley boy," having grown up in Los Angeles's San Fernando Valley and in Hollywood. He holds an advanced degree and has led a varied working life that included being a cosmetologist and teaching in California's community college system. More than a decade ago, his partner's death from cancer ended their 27-year relationship. Today, Norman shares his life with his friend Bud Jordan. They live together in Bud's house three days each week;

the other four days, Norman stays with his partner, Steve Scott, at their home in nearby Palm Desert.

Bill Strong, 66, of Sewanee, Tenn., grew up in Cleveland as one of seven children. He was married there and with his wife raised a family of seven children before filing for divorce in 1983. Bill was an optician for 25 years, and he owned and operated a lens and glasses dispensary for 12 years in Ohio. After his divorce, he migrated to the South, where he supported himself as a home handyman and a Fuller Brush salesperson. He officially retired in 2000 but still keeps a few customer accounts. In Tennessee, Bill met his longtime partner, who is a decade younger than he, and they settled in the university town of Sewanee, population 2,100, where they have lived together for the past 17 years. Bill describes his adopted hometown as liberal, although it's in "the heart of the Bible Belt."

Will Belais, 65, of Washington, D.C., is a retired college professor who taught theater for 30 years. He is now involved in making training films for law-enforcement agencies, including the FBI. He grew up in Virginia, living in both rural and urban areas, and has an identical twin brother and two sisters. Married at 27, Will has two children. He and his wife are now legally separated, although they still remain married. Will is extremely active in Washington's gay and lesbian community: He sings in the Gay Men's Chorus, works for the annual gay and lesbian film festival, belongs to the local gay chamber of commerce, and leads his church's welcoming outreach program. He owns a northwest Washington town house that he shares with a housemate. An Internet enthusiast, he continues to seek his life partner and new friends online.

Dave, 65, of Tamarac, Fla., spent most of his life in the New York City area. Wed at 21, he raised a family there and worked for many years as an accountant, retiring in 1994. While he was married, Dave met his life partner, who was then also married with children. Four years ago, Dave divorced his wife after 40 years of marriage, and he and his life partner subsequently moved to South Florida. At that time their relationship had already lasted 23 years, through both of their marriages, the death of his partner's wife, and Dave's divorce. They may relocate again, however, because of mixed feelings about where they now live.

Jack, 65, of Wilton Manors, Fla., grew up in Texas and holds a Ph.D. in a scientific field. Though he retired in 1997, he continues to do some consulting work. He and his partner of 39 years, Bob, met in college and have been together ever since. They reside in a waterfront town house in Wilton Manors, the nation's second city (after West Hollywood, Calif.) to elect a city council with an openly gay and lesbian majority. Surrounded by Fort Lauderdale, Wilton Manors has a population of 11,000. Jack and Bob estimate that the neighborhood where they have lived for two years is 40%–50% gay and lesbian.

Rod Harrington, 65, lives on his farm near St. Joseph, Mo. He was born on a farm less than a mile away. Other than political work, the demands of grain farming occupy much of Rod's time. During the growing season, his day begins at dawn and doesn't end until sundown. He prepares the soil, plants corn and soybeans, cultivates the crops, sprays for pests, and keeps the fields clear of weeds. At the end of each growing season, he harvests and markets the crop yield. Now divorced, Rod was married for 24 years and has a son. An advocate for gay and lesbian issues, Rod volunteered in a successful effort to keep a Colorado-style antigay amendment from reaching the Missouri ballot.

Norm Self, 65, of San Diego is an ordained United Methodist minister. Twice married but now divorced from both of his wives, Norm is a program leader for Body Electric, the Oakland-based organization devoted to teaching people "how to connect with deeper centers of pleasure in their bodies" by means of "erotic exploration of the mind, body, and heart." The holder of four university degrees, Norm is a lifelong worker for social justice. He is also a veteran of two tours in the U.S. Navy—one as an enlisted man, the other as an officer. He has also trekked through Nepal. He likes being 65 years old and retired, and he looks forward to the "prospect of getting older."

Bill Worrall, 65, of Palm Desert is a native Canadian who was raised as one of seven children in London, Ontario. He still works full-time as a corporate purchasing agent. Before coming to the United States, Bill had served in the Canadian Air Force. He is the founder and president of Prime Timers of Greater Palm Springs, a nonprofit social organization for mature gay men. Now single—his partner died 16 years ago—Bill is optimistic about forming another long-term relationship. He is a computer enthusiast and an avid denizen of the Internet.

CHAPTER 1
Who We Are

LIFE RIGHT NOW

"I'm just on top of the world. I'm totally delighted; I'm having a great time. The best part of my life is right now, unless I look ahead—and I think that's going to be better."

—Norm Self

Many of the men interviewed for this book are, like Norm Self, quite happy with their lives, often because they finally feel free to live on their own terms. Tom Pait says, "I feel good. I do exactly what I want. I have a few close friends whom I do things with, go to the theater with, take trips with. To me, my life is very interesting." Likewise, Robert Bettinger states, "It's an enjoyable time of life. I'm 72 and healthy, able to do whatever I want." Ed Conlon says, "I am at the point in my life that probably is the most rewarding because I can plan my life as I want, do what I want, put my life in any direction I want." Some of the men have an almost spiritual take on this newfound freedom. Milton Lestz, for example, sees himself as a man on a journey: "Where the journey will lead me I am not sure, but it's a very interesting and wonderful journey."

Some of the men, though, have concerns. Bill Worrall rates his life at "about a 7 on a scale of 1 to 10" because he is single. "Life would probably be better if I had a partner," he says. Ed of Oakland, while satisfied with his life, is concerned about the memory problems his partner, Bob, is experiencing. Ed worries that Bob's condition "may cast a shadow over our relationship of 55 years." And Jack, though he describes his life as "very good," acknowledges that he is addressing "some problems" by seeing a psychologist. Will Belais says, "I was teaching for 30 years, then I retired. My income dropped considerably. I thought I had things under control financially, but right now I'm in a bit of a turmoil." José Sarría has an interesting take on things: "Life right now is going faster than I want it to go. It seemed that I was never going to get old. And now it seems that I'm never going to be young again."

Growing Up and Family Life

"I had a loving family in which you did not go to bed at night unless you kissed your mother and father good night. You did not leave the house unless you kissed them goodbye, and you did not come in without embracing them."

—*Ed Conlon*

Many of the men found growing up to be a happy time. Richard Malloy, an only child, recalls "a perfect, happy, and beautiful childhood—tremendous. No nymphomaniacs, no alcoholics, no child molesting, no abuse—absolutely perfect." For Virgil Hylton, growing up on a small farm near Willis, Va., as one of five children "was a happy time." Frank Poe, who grew up in Tennessee with a twin brother, recalls his early years fondly. "There was nothing wrong with any part of growing up. My mother supported me in most things. She was very gentle in telling me what I should be doing instead of what I was doing. My father took us everywhere. We went to every state park—all over the place, even to Canada to see the Dion quintuplets when I was 16. On the trip to Canada I remember that I knew how to drive a car and wanted to, but my dad wouldn't let me."

For others, childhood was less enjoyable. John Schiappi, who grew up in Ithaca, N.Y., says, "If we had known then what we know now, my mother would have been classified as clinically depressed. She went through several serious bouts of bedridden depression." A major component missing from John's childhood was affection. "There was no sign of physical affection between my mother and father or between parents and the children. My sister…committed suicide in her early 30s. Her death was one of the more traumatic experiences of my life."

Most of the men interviewed, however, remember childhood as a mixed bag. Mel Clark recalls his troubled boyhood on a Missouri farm about 80 miles west of St. Louis: "My mother, who died at a relatively early age, was sort of a bitch and gave my father a lot of problems. I remember them fighting when I was a child. I was sick a lot, and I grew up with a very strong inferiority complex." Mel now attributes his early feelings of inferiority to a mistaken view of his rural background. "I grew up on the farm and considered myself poor, although we really weren't." Mel's relationship with his family took a turn for the better after his mother died and his father remarried. "I have a wonderful stepmother," Mel boasts.

"She's now 87 and in a nursing home. I'm her guardian, and I handle her affairs and take care of her."

Ben Fowler's recollection of his early life in Ardmore, Pa., is similarly ambivalent. "My mother was very strict. Black is black; white is white. Children ought to be seen and not heard. You ate what was put in front of you, or you went to bed hungry. My father was a very loving, caring individual. I'd had a heart murmur ever since I was 2, so I was overly protected and not allowed to participate in sports. I went to private school for the first six years, but when the Depression came along I was sent to public school."

Some of the men had rather unusual childhoods. Jim Edmonds, for example, recalls being raised with three sisters in a religious African-American family in a western New England town. "We grew up in a white neighborhood in Pittsfield, Mass., population 50,000. All the blacks lived in one section of town except for my [immediate] family, my grandparents, and my cousin's family. The black church was in a white neighborhood, and my great-grandfather was the first minister of that church. I don't know if that's why we lived in a white neighborhood."

Cyprian Fary's early years were jolted by World War II. He grew up with two brothers and one sister in a small farming village in what was once part of Czechoslovakia. "There was nothing [in the village], really, besides the church, city hall, two stores." He recalls his early years during World War II. "When the war started, I was only 5 years old. When the Germans came in, they took everything from us; the horses and tractors—everything they took away from us. So we had to do everything by hand. We had to take a shovel and shovel everything by hand, plant everything by hand too. So it was kind of a hard time in one way, but a happy time because the family was all together, working."

Ed Conlon, an only child, spent the first six years of his life on a barge on the Hudson River in Jersey City, N.J. "We docked at a grain elevator that loaded our barge with wheat and barley, rye, malt, flax seed, and then we would be towed to other grain elevators…to unload into the flour mills. My family life was…very limited: a father, a mother, a man I was named after, and other men who were barge captains. I didn't have playmates." Ed believes he developed a strong sense of "fantasy and imagination" because of his isolation from his peer group. "Comics were read to me. I remember them so vividly. My memory of [being] 3, 4, and 5 years old is being on the barge with the comic characters Dick Tracy, Buck Rogers, Flash Gordon. The men [working] on the barge built a park for me on the tidelands [with] shores, ponds, and pools. In this park were vines from trees I swung from [and] wildflowers and butterflies. I grew up in this secluded world of my own in an adult community and with an adult mentality. When we moved from the barge to the city, it was difficult for me…to relate to children my own age. I found many of the children childish. I didn't want to play tag; I couldn't see the point of it. I shied away from sports because I had never had to be competitive, and sports were competitive."

Some of the men recall a feeling of isolation during childhood. Rod Harrington poignantly remembers how his parents "weren't happy with each other" while he was growing up on a farm in northwest Missouri. "My mother didn't socialize easily. My playmates were limited. It was a lonely time." On a somewhat happier note, Bill Strong recalls growing up as one of seven children in a poor family in Cleveland. "We were a close family and didn't have a lot of contact with the outside." Still, he says, "it was a happy time for me because of the closeness of the family. The family was the center; I did not have a lot of outside friends."

Many of the men grew up poor. John Peters' father was unemployed for much of the Great Depression. Bill Worrall's father, a low-income Canadian postal worker, managed to support a wife and seven children. Bill also notes, "My father was in World War I and had survived a mustard-gas attack." The man would suffer from health problems related to his wartime injury for the rest of his life.

Bud Jordan says of his childhood, "We lived poor. Our neighbors were poor. We were tobacco farmers and depended on the December sales to get a little money together." Bud lost his mother when he was 3 years old. His two brothers, who were age 4 and 8 at the time, shared in the loss. After the mother's death, the family was forced to a break up. "It was during the [Great] Depression. We were poor, poor farmers, and we lost everything. My father moved to Cincinnati from Kentucky to find a job." During the year it took Bud's father to find employment, the three boys "were loaned out to different people in Kentucky. I stayed one place; one brother stayed with an aunt, the other brother with another relative." When the father finally found employment, the boys were reunited with him. Bud's father subsequently "met a friend" in Cincinnati. "He married her. She took us in; she had two children, and then my father lost his job. By then there were many kids and only one person working. Thirty dollars a month is what we lived on."

Mike, like Bud Jordan, also lost a parent at age 3—his father—though his family was not forced to split up or endure crushing poverty. "My mother took over. I have two brothers and two sisters, and we get along pretty good. My brother and I always fought, because I was the baby of the family and I got most anything I wanted. I was spoiled."

Despite the backdrop of the Great Depression, several men did not experience poverty growing up. Ed of Oakland, who was raised just south of Minneapolis, characterizes his boyhood as a "traditional Midwest middle-class experience. We had a lake house in the summer." Sometimes his family traveled east "to visit relatives in New England."

John Peters and Steve Scott come from the largest families of origin among the interviewees. John was one of a Midwest brood of 12 children that has since whittled "down to three" survivors. Steve grew up in Utah and was the youngest of 13 children born to a Mormon farming family. "I was always the baby, a 'change of life' baby. My parents were like my grandparents. I always believed I was happy, and I was. But later, in therapy, I realized that my childhood was quite fucked up. The farm…was so far out in the country that I couldn't go to high school. I had to go away to high school for the whole nine months every year."

RACE AND ETHNICITY

"My father's mother came over from England, and my father was just a plain American man."

—*Frank Poe*

The 41 men interviewed for this book represent an ethnic mix emblematic of the American melting pot. Most can trace their ancestry to the British Isles or continental Europe. Two are African-American, one is multiracial, one is Latino, and two are part Native American. The men were not questioned about any feelings they have about their ethnicity, since the focus of this book is on aging.

Robert Tingling, who identifies as multiracial, states, "I'm English, I'm Welsh, I'm Chinese, I'm East Indian, I'm African." Jim Edmonds, who describes himself as "Afro-American," is actually a mix of "black, white, and Indian." Steve Scott says his father was "a quarter Cherokee Indian. My [maternal] grandparents were German, [and] my paternal grandmother was English, so I'm sort of a mixture. Legally, you only have to have one-eighth Indian to call yourself a Native American, and that's what I am."

A few men strongly identify with their cultures and nationalities of origin. José Sarría describes his ethnicity as Spanish on both sides of his family. "My father's family were nobles that came from the southern part of Spain." A family castle and lands dating from the 1700s were given to the Franciscan order, he recalls. And "quite a few members of the family were Franciscans." Cyprian Fary states, "I come from Czechoslovakia, [or what] used to be Czechoslovakia, but now it's Slovakia, so I'm from Slovakia." John Kiley, a naturalized American citizen of Australian birth, had "Irish and English parents."

Likewise, although most of the interview participants were American-born, many come from a mix of relatively recent European immigrant parentage. Ed Conlon states, "I had a Hungarian mother, which put me in touch with a gypsy-type family—those that came directly over from Hungary—and a father who was Irish and German." Will Belais says, "Technically, my dad was a Frenchman and my mom is English, so I consider myself a European. I have no trouble with that at all, [even though] I was born in Panama." John Schiappi's mixed parentage is European as well. "My father was born in Switzerland; my mother is of Irish extraction." John Peters says, "My father was Polish, my mother a mixture of German and Dutch, so I'm a real hybrid." Other interviewees have well-entrenched WASP backgrounds. Ed of Oakland, for example, describes all his ancestors as "Anglo-Saxon, from the year of the Norman invasion."

On Knowing We Are Gay

"Oh, God, I think when I was in the cradle. I told my dog when I was 8 years old [that] I was gay. The dog didn't know what I was talking about, and I didn't know what I was talking about either."
—*Richard Malloy*

For many of the men, coming to terms with their gay identity, not surprisingly, was a major rite of passage. For some, the initial realization came very early; for others, it came when they were adults. Whatever their circumstances, the men invariably experienced confusion and emotional turmoil fostered by society's often fiercely antigay attitudes. The path to self-realization and self-acceptance frequently included heterosexual relationships, sometimes even marriage and children. Of the men who once lived as heterosexuals, some were also involved in male/male relationships—even while they were still married and raising children. Sometimes, these same-sex relationships were dismissed as simply a stage, something to outgrow. One way or another, though, all 41 men overcame the prejudices of society and accepted themselves.

Some, like Richard Malloy, feel their sexual orientation is something they've always known about. Others can pinpoint the age at which they became aware of their sexual orientation (an issue separate from self-acceptance). Many did not have gay sex or relationships in their early lives—or if they did, they made no connection between having sex with a man and "being gay." Eleven men say they first realized they were gay between ages 5 and 12. Ten men knew by their early teen years, 9 by their late teens or early 20s. One man claims he knew at age 4; another says he knew at 2. Jack, an only child who grew up in Texas, says he knew he was gay "before there was any terminology for it."

For George Casper, realizing he was gay occurred over a continuum. "By the time I was 13, I knew I was very different in some way from my friends and boys my age. I didn't know what the difference was. Some of the people my age, not my friends, thought they knew what the difference was because they called me 'fairy.' Well, I didn't know what that meant, and I'm not sure they did. By the time I was 16, when I graduated from high school, I understood that I was like all the other boys, except the people I was attracted to erotically and emotionally were men. I had it figured out, but I still didn't know the name for it."

Others share George's experience of knowing he was different but not knowing the word for it. When he was in high school, Rod Harrington was definitely aware that boys "looked better to me than girls, but I didn't have a name for it." Sounding a similar note, Jim of Michigan says, "I always liked men. I didn't realize it [meant that I] was being gay. I was just attracted to other guys." Norman Eckelberger recalls: "There were boys in my class that I was interested in, but I didn't understand why. I almost went to my gym coach to talk to him about it. I didn't, and I'm glad I didn't." Clee remembers that one night his family was sitting around the table when his brother asked their mother what the word *homosexuality* meant. She told him, "Look it up in the dictionary." Tom Pait realized he was gay at age 5 or 6 but adds, "I was just a kid. And there was no name for it in those days. Nobody ever talked about it. I thought I was the only one."

"As far as being gay," admits Bud Jordan, "I didn't know what the word meant, but I have been gay ever since I was out of the womb." Bud had his first gay sexual experience at age 7 or 8 and, when he was 14, had even aroused the sexual interest of another teenage boy. "This guy was putting the make on me, and I liked it. From then on, that's the way it was." He remembers cruising for sexual pickups at parks when he was 16. "I knew [that if I walked] through a park...I might be picked up, but I didn't know the what or why of it. The idea of being gay...didn't enter my mind. I didn't know what the word *homosexual* meant until I was drafted into the Army at 18. I thought it was very odd [when they asked if I was] homosexual. I didn't know what the hell they were talking about. To a guy on the train, I said, 'They asked me that question, and I really didn't know what to say, but I said no, anyway.'"

Mike also remembers that as a young man he didn't exactly know what "being gay" meant. "The first time I actually had a gay experience was at age 21. I was hitchhiking, going to Los Angeles, and this man picked me up. As we were driving along, he offered me a beer, and I drank the beer. The next thing I knew, he started talking about this and that, and then we started talking about sex, and he started putting his hand on my leg. I didn't know what was going on. And then he reached further up my leg until he touched my penis. And then my penis grew, and it felt good. The next thing I knew, he parked, unzipped my fly, took out my cock, and started sucking on it. I enjoyed it. But I didn't think it was me being gay, because I never reciprocated."

Cyprian Fary also first realized he was gay at 20 or 21. "I was like I am now, but I was too young to understand. Even when I was attracted to men and everything, I still did not know the gay idea, because I'd had sex with women, but I never loved them."

Robert of Palm Desert is another man who first tried having relationships with women. He was about 25 before he realized there was something missing in these relationships. "I always dated women, and had sexual relations with women. I was engaged to be married at one time. But about that time I began to notice and admire good-looking men and [at first] was confused as to why. I then realized that I was gay, and I accepted it. If I was to live my life over again, I wouldn't want it any different."

Frank Poe says he knew he was gay at 18 or 19, but "I had to keep that a deep, dark secret. I was dating girls to please my mother. She would introduce me to this or that girl, and I'd date her a couple of times. I didn't reveal to my parents—never did— that I was gay. When I got to California, that was a different story. I met Ed Wright, and we moved in together in Monterey Park [and stayed there] until he died."

Ed of Oakland doesn't believe there was a particular time when he realized he was gay. In high school, he says, he had strong feelings for both sexes. "I made efforts to develop a relationship with girls in my class, but recognized I was not strongly attracted to girls." His first gay experience was in 1935 at age 17, when he went off to college in the East. "I was on a Pullman and changed trains in Chicago. Between trains I went to hear the Chicago Symphony play in Lakeside Park. I was sitting there, and some young fellow came up and started to talk to me, and my train didn't leave for New York until midnight, so I had plenty of time. Before I knew it, he grabbed my crotch and had my penis in his mouth." Ed says, "I was petrified. I spent most of my night running back and forth in the Pullman, washing myself, hoping that my future would be unaffected by this. On the other hand, it was very pleasant."

For John Kiley, who first experienced male-male sex at age 9, there was no gay epiphany. "It sort of just crept up on me. There was no moment when a light bulb went off. I think I was always attracted to men." He is one of several interviewees who seem to have always known they were gay.

Jon Borset says, "I was always kind of an outsider, mainly because of my being gay—not knowing that I was gay, but I knew something was different. And other people knew it too."

Ed Conlon says he was "having sex at the age of 5 and knew what I was doing with my two male cousins, one a year younger, the other a year older. When we would visit my aunt, who lived in the city, sometimes my mother and I would stay over. Naturally, I was put into the bed with my cousins, and we always wound up having sex. How and why, I don't know."

"When I was 4 years old, I knew," says George of New York City. "I don't know why I was precocious about that whole subject, but I was and knew it was a source of shame even at that age. One of the things my mother introduced me to were pictures of saints and religious personalities. And it was remarkable that, even at age 4 or 5, naked saints turned me on. At 10 I can remember consciously forming the idea, 'Oh, God, let this only be a phase.'"

Bill Strong says he would pore over the Sears Roebuck catalog at age 12. "I liked to look at the men in their underwear, or if we happened to get a National Geographic, the unclothed natives, so I knew I was different."

Steve Scott says, "Oh, gosh, I've forever known I was different." He reports that the first time he acted on his sexual desire for other men was between his freshman and sophomore years of high school. "I met this male nurse, and we went to bed. I was staying with an older sister, who was more like an aunt to me. She found out about it and called my parents. To this day I don't know what she told them, but I went back to Utah to school right after that. Another time, in Salt Lake City when I was 16, I met this captain in the Air Force and had this weekend affair." Afterward, once Steve had returned to his relatives in town so he could continue high school, the captain wrote him two love letters—and sent them to his parents' farm. Steve's mother opened the letters and read them, but "she didn't get it. Anyone would [have understood] what was going on except my mother." Steve's father, on the other hand, understood. His only comment, though, was "You'd better be careful."

EDUCATION

"Five years you go to grade school, then three years you go, like, to high school. If I started over again, I would work to have a better education, a higher education."

—*Cyprian Fary on the education he received in Czechoslovakia*

The 41 men interviewed were educated mainly in American or Canadian public schools, though some received all or part of their primary education in private schools, often ones affiliated with religious institutions. A few men attended school in other countries. Nearly all the men earned a high school diploma or its foreign equivalent. A number have four-year college degrees, and several hold advanced degrees. Each man believes that the education he received impacted his later life.

Cyprian Fary says that in his eight years of Czechoslovakian education Russian was the foreign language he studied; there was no English-language instruction Today, he understands Russian "pretty good, but it's already so many years, you know." He views the education he received as minimal compared to what is available now. Robert Tingling, on the other hand, feels the elementary and high school education he received in Jamaica "helped a lot, because when I came [to the United States] I got an associate degree" and later "added more courses at Midwest colleges."

José Sarría, even though he grew up in San Francisco, spoke only Spanish in his early years. His mother wanted him to forsake Spanish in favor of English because he lived in the United States. But José continued to study Spanish in private schools so he would not forget it. After high school and serving in World War II, he attended college in Europe and worked as a Spanish and French translator. When he returned home, José continued his education in Oregon and California and became a Spanish teacher.

Most of the men whose formal education ended with high school are satisfied with the level of education they received. Robert of Palm Desert feels his high school in Grand Rapids, Mich., gave him "great understanding and common sense" that prepared him for "some very good positions in personnel, management, and supervision." Similarly, Bill Strong says he is "very comfortable" with his high school education.

Milton Lestz has a slightly different view. He graduated from high school and attended college but did not graduate. He says, "If I knew then what I know now, I would've finished college. My career would have been different."

Unlike Milton, George of New York City did finish college. He holds an advanced degree with a specialized focus in Western

European economics. He remembers college as a fun time, but he thinks he "stayed too long at the party." He adds, "When I was growing up, you sort of went with the herd going for a four-year bachelors, and then you did a masters. But...I got terribly bored in my third year. If I'd had my druthers, I would have done more in music studies."

Richard Malloy characterizes his education as "weird because, going to Hollywood when I was so young, they didn't know what to do with a Hollywood child in a professional children's school, [so they] pushed me ahead, and I ended up graduating [from] high school at 15. Then I had a scholarship to Kent State University. Did that. Then went on to New York with the Theatre Irvine School with Anne Baxter and a whole group for about three years. I wasn't academic fodder because I knew what I wanted to do at an early age."

Most of the men with collegiate and postgraduate degrees are happy with how their education has impacted their lives. Jack feels that earning a Ph.D. at Johns Hopkins University has opened doors throughout his career and continues to make his life better in retirement because he "can pick and choose" the consulting work he takes on. Robert Bettinger, an ordained Episcopal priest, graduated from Berkeley Divinity School at Yale University and later earned a masters and a Ph.D. in psychology and organizational behavior. He believes his education "was dynamic, enabling me to do lots of things."

Ordained United Methodist minister Norm Self has earned four university degrees, including a Ph.D. He views his education as "crucial to me being who I am. I'm grateful for it, but I temper it with a lot of other things. I think my education tilted me in the direction of a lot of 'headiness,' and my head has sometimes conflicted with my heart, so I've been more analytical and less on a feeling level. Then I kind of bounced over to the other side in the 'touchy-feely' direction for a while, but now I feel good about the balance."

Not all of the men who attended religious schools entered the clergy. Frank Poe says, "I went to a religious-type college in Memphis that mostly had students studying to be ministers. Not me: I went there for four years, got a B.A. in economics." Mike says, "The best education I got was in Catholic school—marvelous. I had nuns, and they just taught us; that was their job. I'm pretty smart actually; I was always in the top 10 in my grade." After eight years of Catholic school, though, Mike transferred to a public high school because "there was no Catholic high school for boys. They weren't allowed in girls Catholic school. Boys were boys, and girls were girls. No coed."

POLITICAL BELIEFS AND VOTING

"I'm certainly a person who believes in diversity and who believes in political action for human rights. I'm not an anything-goes liberal, and I'm definitely not a redneck conservative."

—*Robert Bettinger*

It is well-documented that older Americans vote with greater regularity than any other age group. Of the 41 men interviewed, only one who is eligible to vote does not do so regularly. Typical of those who vote, Bob says, "I've never missed an election." Jim

Mitchell says, "I haven't missed an election since I was eligible to vote." George Casper calls politics "his favorite indoor sport." John Peters sees himself as "more politically active today" than ever before and is a regular poll worker. He adds, "I am a member of the Older Iowa Legislature. Every year I get selected to be a cochair of various committees, and I really do enjoy it."

Norm Self says, "One of the good things I got from my papa was an appreciation for social justice and the political process. Some of his champions were John L. Lewis, the leader of the coal miner union [United Mine Workers of America] and Franklin Roosevelt and the New Deal. My political teeth were cut on Democrat politics in what was the only Republican county in the whole South at that time. I've always had a propensity toward social justice." He adds, "I don't think I've ever missed [voting in an election]."

Ed Conlon is also a regular voter in every primary and general election. "I resent anyone that does not use the privilege to vote," he says. "I see so many of my friends who complain, get on a soapbox, and then sit on their ass and do absolutely nothing to better the community." Conlon recalls how he became an activist relatively late in life at age 54: "Prior to that...I sat on a barstool and did nothing but enjoy a social life. I entered a silly contest. The bar Bee Jay's was running a contest to elect their first king and queen. Guess who won the queen title. The bar owner, Clint Johnson, said I had to represent them as 'Queen Eddie.' My 'coronation' was just as AIDS first came upon the scene. I had to go out and do fund-raising for AIDS. This introduced me to a community I had not been part of. Fortunately, that community accepted me. The more I got involved, the more I became politically aware. And that's when I learned the strength of politics, because we started to elect gay people into city and state government."

Rod Harrington also became involved in gay politics when he was in his 50s. "When you come out as late as I did, after dealing with marriage, you decide you want to give something back. I got involved in politics as a gay man at the state level. I was very involved in opposing the Colorado-style anti–gay rights amendment here in Missouri that never even got out of the petition stage."

John Schiappi, otherwise a lifelong voter, became disenchanted with the Democratic Party and its leaders and skipped the 1996 presidential election. "I declined to vote, having gotten fed up with Mr. Clinton. In the District of Columbia, you can indulge yourself in that sort of thing. I would have voted if I had been in Maryland or Virginia."

Lee Denman is the only U.S. citizen among the 41 men who doesn't vote. "I got out of the habit when I was living overseas and [have] never registered since I returned."

Most of the men identify politically as either liberal or middle-of-the-road. George Casper says, "I think anybody who knows me would call me liberal. I hate the labels, but that communicates how I am easier than anything else." Robert Bettinger also hates the term *liberal* but says, "That fits more than anything else." Ed Conlon states, "I definitely am not conservative. I feel I would be middle-of-the-road to liberal." Mel Clark describes himself thus: "Conservative in some aspects, like finances, but I'm liberal on [the] needs of people. I don't really belong to [either group]. I'm middle-of-the-road."

Not surprisingly, family history sometimes plays into the men's political leanings. Mike says, "I'm a Democrat. I've always been a Democrat, like most people in South Boston. If you were born in South Boston, you were a Democrat." Jon Borset comes from a "pretty staunch" Republican family. "I kind of picked that up," he says, "but I switched after I became aware of things and became more liberal." Ed of Oakland says of his political bent, "Depends on the issue. I'm a good Democrat, but I have lots of ambivalence about some of the issues under discussion. My family was Republican. My grandmother was a Republican national committeewoman. My father was a businessman, almost a right-wing person. Politics was a very important part of our life because we lived in a very active political community."

José Sarría made perhaps the boldest political move of any of the men: He ran for San Francisco city and county supervisor in 1961. José describes himself as the first openly gay man to run for political office in the United States. "I'm the first gay person that said, 'I am gay and I am running for public office. It's my right.' I put my bid in. There were five offices open, and nine people were running. About 10 hours before candidate filings closed, the city fathers of San Francisco got nervous because I boasted that there were 10,000 voting gay people. They said, 'Oh, that's bullshit,' because they never paid attention and because gay people always thought they were second-rate citizens. I never have. The city fathers said, 'You know, maybe he is right. We've got to do something about this.' So they went out, and they got a total of 33 people to run. It didn't bother me. We were registering people to vote and doing our thing. I was running to let people know we have the right to run. I came in ninth. I think I'd have died, had I won." José never ran for office again but says, "I opened the door. From that day on, nobody ran for anything in San Francisco without knocking on the door of the gay community."

SELF IMAGE

"I think I'm a bright and lively 70-year-old who enjoys a lot of things about life. I'm sometimes an old man. I'm single at this moment, so I'm sort of in an emotionally vulnerable place."

—*George Casper*

Most of the men have accepted themselves for who and what they are. A few are concerned about aging, but most are happy with their lives. Clee says, "I'm proud of myself. I think people like me. I mix well. I'm generally content with 'me' now." Jim Edmonds says, "I've accomplished a lot in the world." Virgil Hylton sees himself as "single, old, enjoying life, in good health, and loving myself." He thinks a sad reality is "that lots of people are neither loved nor lovable." Ben Fowler sees himself as an introvert who didn't like himself for a lot of his life, "but I am a very outgoing person now and try to share my enthusiasm for life." Norman Eckelberger says, "I'm very honest, a good person. I'm very happy in my life." José Sarría states, "I don't feel as old as I am on paper, yet I know I am. I'm slower, but my mind is still fast. I still have goals. Some people at a certain age kind of give up. As for myself, I have not given up."

Charles, however, feels vulnerable. "Well, I'm older now. I'm a little bit apprehensive. We all know that we're on the south side of the mountain, as I call it." Rod Harrington laments, "Physically, I've sort of gone to pot. I've got too much stomach." But he adds, "I have a lot of friends. People come to me, I don't have to seek them out. I'm incredibly blessed that way." George of New York City views himself "as a rather decrepit old guy" compared with his younger self. "I have some pictures of myself when I was younger. I was really a startlingly good-looking guy. I picked one photo up, and I said, 'This is me.' Then I picked up another and said, 'This is me now.'"

Almost none of the men express bad feelings about being gay. Mel Clark says he is "a person who just happens to be gay. I don't put that much emphasis on being gay; it's just natural for me." Jim Mitchell describes himself "as a gay man. My whole adult life I've seen it that way. I've lived it as an out gay person at my job. I was a schoolteacher, president of my teachers' union. The board of education knew I was gay. The administrators knew. The students knew. I never tried to hide anything." Likewise, Bud Jordan has "always felt proud" of being gay. "I have had no qualms with my lifestyle." And John Schiappi is proud that his former employer is listed as one of the "100 best companies for gays and lesbians," largely, he says, because there had been an "openly gay vice president of human resources—namely me." Jim of Michigan sums it up: "Oh, it's a lovely life, being gay."

CHAPTER 2

Money and Making it Last

Is There Ever Enough?

"I think I have enough. I'll find out!"

—*Milton Lestz*

The late Duchess of Windsor once said, "You can never be too rich or too thin." Another adage summarizes the money crunch some older Americans face: "If I [had known] I was going to live so long, I would have organized my money differently."

Because money drives so much of who people are and what they do, its sources and adequacy are crucial, especially to older individuals. The 41 men interviewed are no exception. Though some have a combination of income sources to support themselves in retirement, others rely predominantly on Social Security.

Social Security, signed into law in 1935 by President Franklin Delano Roosevelt, today reaches 44 million Americans. Two thirds of those individuals count on it for half or more of their income, and one third have no income at all beyond Social Security. According to 1996 Social Security Administration data, Social Security benefits account for 65% of the annual income of retirees in the middle income range, $13,000 to $20,000 annually. For retirees in the highest range, $38,000 or more, Social Security accounts for 31% of their income.

Most studies agree that more than half of all U.S. households have saved less money than what is needed for a "comfortable retirement," usually defined as having enough money to maintain a lifestyle close to the household's current one. One study found that half of all Americans have never tried to figure out exactly how much money they will need to maintain their standard of living in retirement. Furthermore, unmarried men and women are less likely to save enough money for retirement than their married counterparts.

Among the men interviewed, though, there is a comfort level and a consensus that they have enough money to live on, although their annual incomes vary widely, from less than $20,000 to more than $70,000. Their sources of income are the same as those of many older Americans: first, Social Security; second, pensions; and third, at least for some, investments. Most of the men are retired, but about one third continue to work either full- or part-time.

When asked about money, John Peters recalls his father's economic struggle during the 1930s. "When I think of how my father raised 12 kids during the Depression, it's beyond my comprehension. I had my hands full with one and wasn't hard hit for money. My father had trouble keeping a job during the Depression. I remember vividly when he finally found [steady] work." He says of his current finances, "I wish I had more [money and] that I had saved better than I did." Fortunately, John receives a "residue of pension" from his deceased wife. "But the wife's pension is strictly savings," he explains. "I never touch that. As long as Social Security stays going, I'm in good shape."

Bill Strong's annual income is approximately $15,000. "So long as Social Security holds up, I'm very comfortable," he says. "I have a Social Security check, and I have a little investment. When I have money left over at the end of the month, I invest it in the stock market or mutual funds." He also reinvests any investment income: "I don't draw from it."

Ed of Oakland is quite happy with the joint annual income he shares with his partner, Bob—approximately $70,000 from Social Security, retirement funds, and investments. He recalls the decision they made as a "family unit" to move into a lifetime-care residence 16 years ago: "Bob and I made the decision to come to live in this city. It's the best present we could give our families so they wouldn't have to worry about us."

With an annual income of approximately $30,000, Norman Eckelberger also enjoys his financial independence. "This is the first time in my life that I've ever been self-sufficient," he says. "I don't have the most money in the world, but I don't have to worry about getting help from anybody else."

Fred and Clee would like to have more money beyond their combined annual income of about $40,000. Clee was in business for himself and retired without a pension but has Social Security and modest investments. Fred also receives Social Security and investment income as well as a small pension. They are quite aware of the value of their hilltop San Francisco home, with its commanding view of the city and the bay, and they "look to the value of their real estate" as a future financial bulwark.

Ben Fowler, a military officer for 20 years, is "very happy" with what he has to live on: "between $30,000 and $40,000 a year." Besides Social Security and military retirement benefits, Ben has savings. "My wife and I were very frugal people, and we had good savings." He also received an inheritance from his parents.

Mike also receives military retirement benefits. He is happy living on between $20,000 and $30,000 annually. "I live good, because I'm single and I live alone. I've got Navy retirement, another retirement from where I worked, and Social Security. I've got money in the bank."

With an annual income of less than $20,000, Bud Jordan still manages to save money. "My partner of 42 years and I saved money. We bought and sold property; we owned rentals; we invested in stock. We struggled and saved and scrimped—both of us worked all the time—so we saved enough. I'm going to make it last." He reluctantly adds, "I hesitate to go into my savings, but know I'm going to have to do it."

Robert Tingling also doubts that his income, under $20,000 a year, will last his lifetime. "I don't know what I will do if I get sick and have to worry about money," he says. "When you get up in your 70s, there are certain things that come around that would not have come around earlier, or you did not expect them to come around."

Jim of Michigan has the opposite problem of most of the men. "I recently inherited a lot of money and am having a bit of a problem dealing with it. Inheriting half a million dollars is something I never had to deal with before."

Ed Conlon perhaps sums it up best. He sees his income as "able to support my needs." He adds, "I would like to have additional monies, but I've always been the grasshopper instead of the ant. I've never been that conservative with money, a spendthrift at times and maybe a little selfish in doing what I've wanted with it. I've never really planned for the future or for security. Now, being retired and with my lover being retired, we can afford what we want to do. We eat well. We can still play well and enjoy our lives without worry."

SPENDING PRIORITIES

"With the years, the number of things I want decreases, which is a very wonderful thing, because you've got all your stuff. My overriding philosophy is to simplify."

—George of New York City

Living on a limited income means that spending must be prioritized. The men interviewed tend to focus on necessities first. Jim Mitchell says he spends his money on "the normal things. I have a mortgage. Food, heat, car. I usually travel once or twice a year." In addition, he supports his ward, a disabled 31-year-old man who lives in Appleton, Wis. Jim's regular trips from his home in Putnam County, N.Y., to visit his ward in Wisconsin increase his expenses considerably.

Will Belais also continues to support a dependent. "My spending priorities right now seem to be taking care of my ex-wife and my house. I'm responsible for my wife—period. I take care of her. She has no income." This arrangement has significantly strained Will's budget. "I've been forced to make my medical bills the third priority. After that, everybody else just has to stand in line."

George of New York City says, "Food, shelter, and some recreation constitute the three biggest spending elements.... Recreation might be going to [New York City's] Jupiter Symphony on a Monday afternoon, or having dinner with friends on the weekend, or going to movies or plays, but in a moderate sort of way."

Robert Bettinger has "a little money for recreation and clothes sometimes, but mostly I spend my income on food for myself and my partner, and to operate a car."

Not all of the men are so frugal, though. Norm Self says he likes to "give away" money if it's going to be put to a good use. "That's my favorite thing to do. What I really like to do is choose somebody who's on a snag, and money is the only thing standing in the way of some productive road in that person's life."

John Schiappi likes to travel and go out. He says he does "a lot of traveling, a lot of theater, a lot of performing arts, a lot of dining out, a lot of social activity." He also financially helps out his son, who is divorced and has three children. "I give him some assistance, and I hope to increase that as [my son's] children approach college age."

Jon Borset also likes to travel. He describes himself as "an intermediate downhill skier," and he owns a condominium near Lake Tahoe, where the skiing is world-renowned. "I like to ski in the winter. That's not particularly expensive, but it's a luxury." Initially, he had bought the cabin "as an investment" and rented it in the winter but lived there himself in the summer. "But since I retired, I want to use it for myself," he says. "I go up at least one week a month and ski by myself or with friends. There are several resorts in the area. I ski around and just thoroughly enjoy myself."

Wills, Trusts, and Leaving an Estate

"I've lived a very good life. I've done everything that I possibly could do. If I drop dead right now, I'm ready."

—*José Sarría*

Almost to a man, the interviewees believe that "quality of life" is the key issue as they grow older. Most of the men are comfortable with the inevitability of death and have a will or a living trust or both. Many were once married and have children, and they plan to leave all or part of their estate to their direct descendants. Others have made similar provisions for nieces and nephews.

John Schiappi is one of the men who plans to leave an estate. "Fortunately, I'm in a financial situation where I can live my life to the hilt," he says, "and unless something drastic happens in the financial world, there will be money left over for my children."

For couples, the welfare of the partner figures heavily in estate planning. Ed Conlon observes about himself and his partner, Shawne, "Everything we own is joint. You're talking to a married person." Each man has drawn up a will leaving the jointly held estate to his partner. Ed's only biological family links are with "cousins I am not close to." He continues, "Over the years, however, Shawne and I have developed what we call a family of friends: people who for 20 years have shared our holiday dinner table. One friend in particular, in the event something should happen to both of us, would be left our estate."

Fred and Clee have a reciprocal trust with the provision that after they are both gone any remaining resources will go to Fred's brother and sister. Clee adds, "We've also taken care of our funeral arrangements."

Jim Mitchell is writing a will and establishing a trust that names an administrator to dispense funds to benefit his ward because "there's no one else to provide for him." Jim feels an urgency to get the will and trust in place. "I just got a diagnosis that I'm going to go blind. It won't happen until about 10 years from now, but it will happen. I have macular degeneration. At the moment, science has no way of stopping that. My eyesight now is OK. Some days it's blurry, and I can't read; other days it's clear, and I can read. I know I'm going to have to depend on someone else to take care of me, at least in part. So I've been dealing with that. I may move to a condo or co-op and will probably have my ward come live with me. He seems willing to do that."

Norm Self says, "I will leave an estate…to my dearly beloved granddaughters. What I want to do too is benefit an organization or cause that embodies my values. One is the Lesbian and Gay Center in San Diego: I've endowed them. The other one is an avocation of my life, a priority in the way I spend my time, and that is the Body Electric School in Oakland."

Conversely, Bud Jordan says, "If I could, I would spend every penny of it. I would too, if I knew how long I was going to live." Norman Eckelberger has similar feelings. He once talked to his brother about leaving an estate and was told, "Don't worry about leaving any money. Just go out and enjoy yourself."

CHAPTER 3

Work, Leisure, Volunteering

HAPPILY WORKING

"It gets me out of the house and breaks the boredom."

—Virgil Hylton

It used to be that an individual would work for 40 years, then go home and do nothing until he or she died. Contemporary life, however, presents an array of options to older Americans. Many continue to work either full- or part-time. Some even launch second careers. Others fill their time with leisure pursuits and volunteer work.

A 1998 study by the AARP indicated that a rising number of Americans over 65 have chosen to continue working. In 1985, 10.8% of Americans over 65 were still in the workforce; by 1998, that percentage had increased to 11.9%. Before the mid 1980s, the size of the over-65 working crowd had been stable for more than 30 years. But more recent surveys show that approximately three quarters of all Americans over 65 expect to work in their retirement. Four million say they actually would like to work after retiring.

Typically, motivations for working are either "I want to" or "I have to." The latter is often spurred by the realization that most people will need about 70% of their pre-retirement income to live comfortably in retirement. Putting this in dollars and cents, analysts (Yankelovich Partners, 1999) say a person who makes $35,000 a year while working will need $583,000 in savings for retirement.

Rod Harrington's working life is the same as ever. He owns the 745-acre farm he works southeast of St. Joseph, Mo. Working alone, he plants, grows, fertilizes, harvests, and markets corn and soybeans. During the growing season, a typical day starts about 6:30 A.M. and ends about 7:45 P.M., with only a quick lunch break. In winter, Rod's days are more relaxed. "I've seen 30 inches of snow on the ground. If it's a day when the roads are dry, I would be trucking grain into either Atchison [Kan.] or Kansas City. If the roads are slick, or I'm not liking the market at the time, I would maybe spend the day reading, or I might shop, or I might, heaven forbid, clean house."

In contrast, Charles commutes daily from New Jersey to his full-time job in New York City. "I work on Wall Street, and I like my job. Wall Street is very different than it was 40 to 45 years ago. There's a different attitude now." Charles works in a back office, and he never sees or talks to customers. "I just deal in paperwork, moving it from one desk to another."

Bill Worrall combines full-time employment with extensive volunteer work. Bill works as a purchasing agent for a major corporation "five days a week, eight hours a day." During his off-work hours, though, he is heavily involved in a nonprofit organization for mature gay and bisexual men and their admirers: Prime Timers. "There were 31 members of Prime Timers of the Desert when I became the [chapter's] first officer. In 10 months, I got the membership up to 817, the biggest in the country and in the world." When the chapter's membership hit 1,000, Bill became vice president and later president of Prime Timers Worldwide. "I've started four chapters, but I'm happiest with this one where I've kept the membership low intentionally with 300 members."

Working provides about three fourths of Mel Clark's annual income. "I was a general contractor in New Mexico for 10 years, doing residential and light commercial design, remodeling, and construction. Then I came back East in '84." After attending to some personal and family obligations, Mel decided he wanted to go back to work. "So I formed a corporation and applied for my contractor's license in Maryland—a long procedure: a lot of paperwork—but I have my license now." During the license waiting period, he did some construction work on neighbors' homes as well as on his own house.

John Kiley is in the process of selling his New York–based company and transitioning to a part-time role in its operation. "I'm working part-time to keep in touch with the industry I've been in for so many years," he says. "I've always liked to work in a place where I'm surrounded by business friends, and I have lots of friends in my industry in the office. It's all sort of an extended family."

Will Belais is technically retired but is still supporting his wife and needs to supplement his retirement income. Therefore, he works for what Washingtonians nickname a "beltway bandit," a subcontractor that takes on projects "government agencies don't do well or don't want to do." Will is involved in making films used by law-enforcement agencies to teach role-playing. The FBI Academy and U.S. Drug Enforcement Administration number among the organizations that use the films in day-to-day training. "I hire actors [and] maintain their payrolls," Will explains. "I was hired because I have a background in theater."

Virgil Hylton says he has a comfortable retirement income that he believes will last his lifetime. He enjoys working part-time, four days a week staffing the entry gate at a nearby retirement community, because he enjoys it. He believes the job makes his leisure time more enjoyable: "reading, relaxing, and lots of cleaning," Virgil also volunteers at the county AIDS childrens task force.

George Casper, a retired civil engineer, also works because he enjoys it. Almost every day, he is at his sister's travel agency, where he markets travel packages to gay men. He does it mostly because he has fun "making new acquaintances and new friends." The travel work can come in spurts because occasionally he has to make complicated arrangements for groups, and that can translate into a high workload, if only temporarily. "The high activity tapers off, and I return to a more leisurely mix of time," George says.

Lee Denman has taken a part-time job since he retired because he was "somewhat bored with everything quiet." He adds, "I ran across an ad looking for someone retired to help out in a home business, and I took it on. Once a week I mind the office while the owner travels."

Jim Edmonds spends four to five weeks every year judging student piano-performance competitions. "It keeps me in contact with my colleagues," he says. When judging competitions, he typically spends each week "hearing [as many as] 350 kids play the piano." Jim has also toured as a pianist throughout the Pacific Northwest and given recitals as far away as Australia.

George of New York City describes himself as semiretired while working part-time as an investor relations consultant. His consulting work brings in about 20% of his yearly income. "I currently have one good client," he says, "a company attempting to play at a stage they're quite ready for." George sees his services as helping the company find an appropriate and realistic niche.

Ed Conlon says, "When I worked full-time, I managed an antiques complex. Now I just baby-sit it part-time, never more than three days a week, say 11 to 5. I greet and talk to people and sell. It takes me out of the house and puts me in touch with people, makes me active. It's not tiresome." As Queen Eddie, Ed has been writing a weekly social column as well as a biweekly advice column for a San Diego gay paper for more than a decade. "Dealing with a deadline every week can be quite frustrating," Ed admits. "I will spend maybe eight hours at a table compiling the social column. The advice column is different: I receive letters from the public and answer them." Nevertheless, he maintains, "I never think of it as work."

Ed describes his drag persona Queen Eddie as "a combination of Mae West and Auntie Mame. She [Queen Eddie] turned into everybody's aunt or grandmother—an older person…that young people feel they can confide in, ask questions, and get advice from." Ed's work as Queen Eddie has slowed since he was diagnosed with cancer, but he is still a regular at Pride parades and fund-raisers. "I think it's very important that the persona of Queen Eddie is out there. That persona—Queen Eddie, senior citizen, 72—still doing things, respected for it, and not limited by age."

Happy Not Working

"I like to go to my church every morning. If I don't have anything special to do, I kind of goof off for a while. I usually go to the public library to use the Internet and read the paper. At noon I go to senior meals. Afterward, I usually get my walk in the afternoon. I try to do at least two miles every day."

—*John Peters*

Among those not working are a number of early risers who spend their mornings in vigorous exercise. Tom Pait is up early and out for a morning run of several miles every day, followed by "breakfast, listening to the radio, and reading the paper." His friend Jon Borset works out at an athletic facility at least four or five mornings per week. Later, the two of them may get together for the numerous street fairs and other activities in their downtown San Francisco neighborhood.

Robert of Palm Desert rises at 5:30 A.M. and is in the pool by 7, frequently with his friend Cyprian Fary. Then they share breakfast, perhaps followed by shopping or a casino visit. Milton Lestz also swims as part of his health regimen. "The first thing in the morning is prayer, then the abs machine." After eating "a very healthy breakfast" and making routine phone calls, he does "water aerobics" and later goes to the gym.

In the early morning Ed of Oakland and his partner, Bob, take a 3.5-mile walk around Lake Merritt, just beyond the front entrance of St. Paul's Towers. "Then we come in, read the paper, and go down to breakfast," Ed says. "Bob usually goes into the garden afterward, and I may handle some business and make fund-raising phone calls. In the afternoon we take a nap, read, whatever. Then it's time for a cocktail, followed by a table for four or six in our dining room. We get to bed early, usually by 9 or 9:30 P.M."

Norm Self is still "getting used to being on paid vacation" for the remainder of his life. "I get up early, even though I don't have to. I like to turn my hand to whatever presents itself. It might be purging the garage, my files, or library, maybe getting rid of stuff. I like connecting with friends, going out to lunch, spending time at the gym. Those are routine 'at home' days. And then I get on the road to Oakland and spend a couple of weeks helping out in the office of Body Electric where I coordinate workshops and do recruiting and logistics."

Though retired, John Schiappi continues to apply his considerable editorial skills to freelance projects. "Typically, I'll spend the morning reading or working on my computer, handling E-mail, and doing research," he says. "I do pro bono work and help friends with projects. I love research and writing. That's the morning. If the weather is good, I go biking for an hour or two and have lunch outdoors. All my life an afternoon nap has been a high priority. Evenings are something social: bridge, theater, or whatever. And I have learned to thoroughly enjoy quiet evenings alone at home."

Not all of the men are early risers. Warde Laidman says, "My mornings consist of reading the paper. After 10 o'clock, I do some physical exercises for approximately an hour. In the afternoon, more reading. My partner and I may go to a movie."

Several men devote their days to leisure and unhurried exercise. Jim Mitchell gets his exercise by walking around the local mall. "If the weather's good, I go to a nice park right near where I live," he says. Jim also makes trips to New York City for theater and concerts. He likes to "come in for a weekend or a few days and stay at a hotel." Beach resident Mike follows an equally relaxed program. "I get up in the morning; I exercise. But I don't eat breakfast until about 10:30. In the summertime I go to the beach [and stay] all afternoon. Lunch on the beach is two cookies. When I come home from the beach in the evening, I shower and eat supper, maybe a TV dinner. I'll look at TV and fall asleep."

George of New York City reads *The New York Times* every day "for the market news." Once he has had breakfast, showered, and dressed, George likes "to get some activity going" by taking a walk around his Upper West Side Manhattan neighborhood. "I love to walk in this area and through Riverside Park. Then I set a goal for myself, say going to the Museum of Modern Art or the Metropolitan Museum. I'll either walk or take the subway." An avid reader with a large library, George adds, "I put an awful lot of reading time in."

Bud Jordan is pleased with the relaxed pace of life in Palm Springs. "I'm nuts to live in Palm Springs year-round," he says. He admits his daily routine is "kind of dull. The first thing I do is walk the dog. That's my exercise, then breakfast and TV. After I fix lunch, which isn't much, I may go to the store and then out to dinner with a friend. I go to bed early."

Another Palm Springs–area resident, Steve Scott, struggles with having so much free time. "Leisure time has always been very hard for me. I've always had so much excess energy that I need to be doing something." Consequently, he spends a lot of time engaged in a variety of activities. "I read a lot. I'm not into television or movies. Leisure might be going to brunch, having people in for dinner, going out, or traveling up to the mountains."

José Sarría feels that "one never retires" and views his life as a series of transitions. José began his career at San Francisco's Black Cat Club, working there from the late 1940s until it closed in 1963. José remembers, "At the beginning, I was a host and waited tables. I did cabaret: singing, dancing, and telling stories. By accident, I began doing a travesty on opera Sunday afternoons. I would tell the whole story, play all the parts, and bring other people into the act." After his run for a seat on San Francisco's Board of Supervisors and the subsequent closure of the Black Cat, José found he had "to reorganize" his priorities again. "I think that's when I became a man," he confides. "There was no mama to pay the bills when I couldn't. I had no crutch. I thought I was going to be at the Cat until the end of my life." It was at that time, in 1965, that José founded the Imperial Court system. "I'm the great pooh-bah, the first Empress and the main person of the whole system." Since then, José has traveled the country performing at gay and lesbian events. He has served as Grand Marshal of Pride parades in San Francisco, Albuquerque, and Minneapolis. Now planning a move to Southern California, José describes a typical day: "I get up and shave, do some phoning, planning, and such because I'm moving. Then I shop for packing boxes. I am sorting clothes so I can start packing. My roommate will make dinner, and I'll wash the dishes. Let me see, what else do I have to do? Oh, a 4 o'clock tea-and-cookie break."

The Satisfaction of Volunteering

"Half my life is volunteering. I've raised money for big projects, for breast cancer, to feed people. I sing and dance, collect the money, and make sure everything's aboveboard."

—*José Sarría*

With the onset of AIDS, gay and lesbians in the United States and elsewhere became a society of volunteers banding together to care for people affected by HIV/AIDS and other serious conditions. Among the men interviewed, San Francisco friends Tom Pait and Jon Borset set a stellar example as volunteers. Together they volunteer for the Bay Area's Project Open Hand, a meal preparation and delivery service for people with AIDS-related and other major illnesses. Tom says that he and Jon "do deliveries down through the Tenderloin. And sometimes we go to the Diamond Senior Center, where there are a few gays, and help serve lunch." Jon also volunteers several hours each week at Project SHANTI, a caregiver agency for people affected by HIV/AIDS. "I sometimes do shopping, sometimes cleaning, run errands, whatever is needed," he says.

Norm Self does "lots" of volunteer work. "I'm on a team youth outreach program called Common Ground at the [San Diego] Lesbian and Gay Center," he says, "and expect to be doing a lot of liaising with school administrators to get HIV/AIDS education into the schools."

Volunteer work, especially work centering around HIV/AIDS

issues, can be draining and lead to burnout. Lee Denman recalls his experience at a hospice for HIV/AIDS patients. "Every day for over a year, I went to Fraternity House, at that time the only AIDS hospice in this area. I cooked the evening meals and some evenings stayed overnight to hand out medicine, to give the residents of the house a chance to have a little time off. But at the end of a year, I just couldn't take it anymore. It's very difficult, getting to know people and coming to work one day and finding they're gone."

Warde Laidman has also done HIV/AIDS-related volunteer work—with an HIV/AIDS hotline and also delivering meals. Now, however, he is doing work with the Episcopal Church in Oakland. "It's getting to be a gay-friendly church, so there are opportunities there for me to meet people [and] talk to people." He also participates in the Lake Merritt cleanup project. "I live on the shore of Lake Merritt, considered to be the jewel of Oakland. It needs a lot of help and care to keep it clean. I put on my hip boots and go out with others for two or three hours a couple of times a week, walking around and in the lake picking up junk and debris."

Warde Laidman is not the only man interviewed who has turned his volunteer focus to the environment. Robert Bettinger lives on a tidal lagoon and volunteers about 20 hours a week to "assist the rangers with small jobs like clearing paths, checking the bathrooms, giving assistance to people, maybe building a table or bookcase—odd, interesting things like that." And Bob of Arizona, in addition to volunteering as a guide/docent at local museums, has led hikes, designed hiking trails, and assembled a team to cut and lay hiking trails in his city.

Ed of Oakland is also "very much" the dedicated volunteer. Soon after he retired, he established a program designed "to help seniors find their way through the bureaucratic maze to get the help they need." He also assists in raising "money for a special outreach to homeless people in San Francisco as well as those living on a very moderate income who can't afford the rents in this area."

Most of the men who volunteer are involved in gay causes of one sort or another. Milton Lestz, for example, is an active volunteer at Senior Action in a Gay Environment (SAGE) in Fort Lauderdale. "I help with the mailing once a month," he says. "And there's a men's talk group I helped organize, and I keep it running and facilitate the weekly meetings. The talk group is a way for men to meet instead of going to bars."

The Juggling Act

"I don't really have enough time to do what I want."

—*Milton Lestz*

Whether one is still in the working world, volunteering, or merely kicking back and enjoying life, there is never enough time for everything. Many of the men spoke of the stress of combining all their activities into just one life.

Part-time travel agent George Casper doesn't like to feel pressured, but he still experiences work-related stress. "Pressure was always in my work life. Now I shouldn't have to work under deadlines, but I still do. I try not to get overloaded anymore."

Jim Edmonds likes that he can now "say yes or no to any of the work that comes along." But pressures can still arise. He recalls a series of scheduled concerts that were eventually "canceled for different reasons, illness or something," but then rescheduled with a tight rehearsal schedule. "I ended up with two back-to-back concerts in each of two months. I try to avoid that."

Not all of the men, however, feel that stress is a bad thing. John Schiappi talks of the time he asked a woman friend, now 82, what the most difficult thing she faced was when she retired: "She said it was the lack of stress in her life. For those of us who've had careers with a lot of stress, that can be difficult to deal with. So the fact that my life still has moments when I seem to be rushing around and under a bit of stress—it's not bad."

The most common complaint, especially for those men who are still working, is lack of time. For instance, full-time worker Charles says he would "like more leisure time, but on Wall Street the job comes first." He says that for him a day off means "housework, which I loathe. I have two dogs and my house to take care of…. Saturday is [for] laundry, dry cleaning, supermarket shopping—the ordinary things of every household."

New York investment counselor George also wishes his time was comprised of "less work and more leisure. That's what retirement is supposed to be," he says. "I am an omnivore as far as leisure is concerned. I really love to do nothing. To quote Whitman, 'I love to loaf.' All my life, I have been a striver, a hard and diligent worker, but I find now that it's not really in me. I would much prefer to just stare at the ceiling sometimes, let thoughts develop and work inside of me."

George spends about 10% of his time each week volunteering at the Lesbian, Gay, Bisexual & Transgender Center in New York City. "But I want to do other things too," he says. "I'm waiting for my [financial] portfolio to start kicking in more bucks so I can rethink working and give some hours to the library or the Jupiter Symphony or somebody else who needs it. But right now I'm limited to the Center."

Jim Mitchell expresses similar sentiments about needing to volunteer more. "I've decided to do more work at my church where we run outreach programs for the aged and people with AIDS, and a day-care program. I can help in all three."

Rod Harrington's farming life is driven by the seasons. "When it's time to plant, to take care of the crop, or to harvest the crop, I don't plan social activities. Work takes precedence. Outside of that, I have lots of time off. I've told people for several years now that I'm semiretired, not really fully employed, and that's partially true and partially not true."

For Will Belais, work is something he does four hours a day, Monday through Friday. "But I never bring it home," he says, "and my volunteer work is almost every day. The computer consumes much more time than I want it to. It's a monster when it comes to [reading] something like 59 E-mails a day and most are junk. But the computer is how my volunteer work gets started and organized, so it's very important. I [try to] balance everything."

Will is not the only interviewee who spends more time than he would like on the computer. Ben Fowler says, "Right now, I feel I'm addicted to the computer. I'm on Net meetings first thing in the morning and last thing at night, seeing and talking to people all over the world." Similarly, John Schiappi says, "I'm a little concerned that I've overindulged in the computer part. I found the Internet and E-mail fascinating, and perhaps I've spent too much time on that. I'm looking to get back into a better balance."

Most of the men who are not working feel good about their lives and welcome the lack of pressure or stress. Richard Malloy sees his life as "perfect and never rushed." John Peters is "very happy" with the balance in his life and "very seldom" feels stress. Robert Bettinger sums it up: "I don't think about the balance as much as I think about doing what's fun and pleasurable, both in volunteer work and in my other leisure time."

CHAPTER 4

Health and Health Care

CURRENT HEALTH SITUATION

"I bike and I swim. I do 70 sit-ups a day. I stopped smoking in the late '50s."

—Jack

All 41 men interviewed for this book agree that maintaining their health is their number 1 priority. Most feel they are in good health. Mike says, "I'm in good health. I don't take any medicines. I take a multivitamin every day and an aspirin every other day, as recommended by a doctor about 20 years ago. I don't know—the way I'm going now, I could live to be 100. The only thing I hope is that I don't get something like Alzheimer's or Parkinson's. I don't know what I'd do. I'm so independent. I could commit suicide actually, if I had to start depending on people."

Bill Worrall says, "Right now my health is good. My family all lived until their 90s. There's only one case of cancer among my parents' families, no heart attacks. We've just been very healthy stock." Fred and Clee also rate their health as good. Clee says, "I'm not in bed, not in pain," and Fred echoes, "That's the way with me too."

Others are not so lucky. Ben Fowler is concerned that his "health is beginning to deteriorate some," adding that his partner, Lee, "is a great help." Lee makes sure that Ben takes his pills and isn't afraid to speak up whenever he feels Ben's "attitude towards his aches and pains is limiting his life." For his part, Ben's attitude is to "keep going" despite the down moments: "I'm not ready to give up yet." Also undaunted by health problems, Jim Mitchell considers his top priorities to be keeping his high blood pressure and diabetes under control and dealing with gradually losing his sight because of macular degeneration.

Vanity is as much a concern as illness. As Southern belles sometimes lament, "I can control my weight, but I can't control its distribution." Weight is not a concern just for Southern belles. Gay men worry about it as well. John Schiappi says, "I think there should be an organization called '10 Pounds Overweight Anonymous' because I think that many of us spend a lifetime feeling, 'I would like to take off 10 pounds.'"

Not everyone feels a few extra pounds are a bad thing, though. George Casper says, "I'm overweight. That makes me attractive to a big subset of people. I feel good about that." He says there are men who "love my belly and want to rub it. If I didn't have it, I wouldn't be attractive to them, so it's great." Similarly, Bill Worrall has dated men who have told him, "Boy, I wish you had two more inches around the middle." Bill adds, "I'm getting more dates now than I ever did when I was growing up. It's probably because of my weight and the color of my hair." Bill does admit that he has a cholesterol problem, though: "The doctor has me on something to bring that down."

Many of the men spoke of having recently lost weight. Fred says he dropped 30 pounds from 255 to 225. "And ever since I got down there, my system has adjusted to that rate. But about four months ago [while I was] on medication, I ballooned up to 240. Now I'm trying to take it off, and it's much, much more difficult now than when I took it off before."

Mel Clark has lost 20 pounds in the last year on an herbal weight-loss program and vows, "My goal is 20 more." George of New York City has lost a significant amount of weight, despite his six-foot stature. "I've gone from 256 to 196 in the past several years under a doctor's supervision," he says. "I could lose some more weight, but I'd look cadaverous. Right now I feel fine about it."

Health issues have led to weight loss for some of the men. Lee Denman reports that he lost 35 pounds. "I was on the verge of becoming diabetic. One of the ways recommended to me to control diabetes was diet, and the result of the diet was the lost pounds, which didn't hurt me in the least."

Ed Conlon, who has cancer, says, "Two and a half years ago, I weighed 240 pounds, and I was happy with it. I weighed 210 when I graduated grammar school at age 14. I've always had weight, always been chubby. My height was 5 foot 10½. I now have shrunk to 5 foot 7½. Don't ask me where the other three inches went. Due to cancer I now weigh 170 pounds, having lost 50 pounds in one month. I am not happy with my weight at 170. I constantly try to gain weight. I'm used to being a full-bodied figure."

Some of the men interviewed feel they are too thin. Milton Lestz says, "I wish I could gain weight, say 10 to 15 pounds, but there's no way in hell I could do that." Ben Fowler feels he is a "little underweight" as well. "But I've always been rather skinny," he adds.

Most of the men who are happy with their weight follow some sort of exercise and/or dietary regimen. Runners John Kiley and Tom Pait and race-walker Jon Borset are good examples of those who maintain an optimum weight primarily through exercise. Virgil Hylton, who has survived a stroke and prostate cancer, combines a special diet with exercise: "I do daily stretching, weight lifting, and walking, and eat mostly fruits, cereal, and veggies."

DIET AND EXERCISE

"I'm an avid bike rider and walker. If the weather's not good, I go to the gym for the StairMaster and for the weight machines."

—John Schiappi

As any physician will tell you, the keys to good health are a healthy diet and regular exercise. Most of the men interviewed usually eat at home, although a few confess to dining out regularly. The men are split between "meat and potatoes" types and "fruits and vegetables" types. Nearly all the men engage in some form of regular exercise. Walking is the most popular choice, followed by swimming and aerobics. A handful of the men are serious athletes who compete regularly.

Tom Pait counts himself among the healthy eaters; he typically starts his day "with a banana, an apple, or an orange and then oatmeal" and ends it "with salad and pasta." Others follow similarly health-conscious diets, even if they dine out frequently. Jim Mitchell eats out for lunch and at home for dinner. "I eat a variety of food," he says. "I'm not a vegetarian, but I like lots of vegetables. I eat fruit every day. I drink tea and a little coffee." For George Casper, cereal grains and vegetables are a priority. "I don't eat much fruit or dessert," he says. Jim Edmonds is fond of seafood, poultry, and fresh fruit, while Jon Borset likes "lots of rice, pasta, chicken, and vegetables." Milton Lestz acknowledges that he "loves very rich, fatty food" but has abandoned those favorites for "a lot of fruit, vegetables, legumes, and fat-free foods."

A few men are vegetarians. Robert Bettinger follows a diet of no dairy, meat, or sugar, as does Bill Strong. Bill says, "I am a vegetarian and have been since my first heart attack in 1990. I gradually closed out red meat and poultry. Occasionally now I have fish."

Just as many of the men are good ol' boy red-meat eaters. Ben Fowler eats meals of "basic meat and potatoes" mostly at home. Mike doesn't "eat out at all" and likes "fried chicken and steak." Rod Harrington, another "meat and potatoes" guy, eats out about three quarters of the time. "I was raised on Mid-America food: meat and potatoes, with vegetables," he says. "My mother was a home economics teacher, so there was a better-than-average attention to nutrition." Frank Poe dines on "mostly TV dinners" at home and "meat, chicken, and fish" whenever he goes out to eat.

Norman Eckelberger says, "Since I'm half-Italian, I love Italian food, and I try to eat the food of my childhood as much as possible." Ed Conlon likes Italian food as well. He would like to eat out more often, but his partner, Shawne, usually says, "'You cook so well: Why should we go out and eat?'" Ed adds, "He [Shawn] doesn't realize how much I enjoy being waited on and the pleasure of a variety of foods, rather than the entrée I cook and serve."

José Sarría likes good food but was brought up to eat everything on his plate. "We were a very cosmopolitan family," José remembers. "No such thing as 'Oh, I don't like that.' No, no, no. You tasted it. Some things you liked more than others. I never did like turnips and parsnips, but I eat them now because I found new ways of cooking them. I've traveled the world, so I've eaten a lot of things that many people wouldn't eat."

For working off the calories, walking is by far the men's preferred physical activity, and it ranges in intensity from leisurely to vigorous. Lee Denman, who lives half a mile from the beach, says, "I try to go down to the beach every morning and walk along the shoreline for a mile or so." He admits he drives to the beach, though, since "the walk back home is all uphill."

John Peters walks two miles daily. At first he walked with a group, but now he does it alone. "They changed the time from afternoon to morning," he says, "and that didn't work out for me because of my volunteer work." Likewise, George of New York City walks "a great deal," adding that he also climbs "every stair I can." Warde Laidman does "very fast walking and sometimes a little jogging around the lake."

Ed of Oakland walks with his partner, Bob, every day. "I walk three and a half miles a day. Bob and I walk as much as we can, and Bob is even more active than I am. I started walking with my grandfather when I was a child, after church on Sundays. [When I was] in school I walked, and when I lived in New York I always walked." Another couple who regularly take strolls together are Fred and Clee. "We have a route that we walk," says Fred. "It's one mile, and we do it nearly every day, rain or shine." Clee chimes in, "We once worked in the garden, but all the bending-over has stopped us."

The next most popular exercise among the men interviewed is swimming. Robert of Palm Desert says, "I'm not a swimmer, but I do swim. I do water aerobics. I like the water and do the backstroke and dog paddle most every day for about a half and hour, and I use a bicycle." Bud Jordan swam every day before getting "a rash from too much sun," but misses swimming and plans to return to the pool. Norman Eckelberger swims every day and does "exercises at night before I go to bed." Milton Lestz does "water aerobics every morning except Saturday and Sunday." Under the supervision of an instructor, he spends "an hour doing physical exercise in the water." Milton says, "I used to play tennis every morning, but don't do that anymore because of my sciatica. Now I go to the gym three times a week and lift weights. Afterward, I sit in the whirlpool bath, shower, and then go home and take a nap."

Combining a variety of physical activities works well for many men. Jon Borset follows a regimen of gym workouts, bicycling, and walking. "In the gym I work on my legs and cardio conditioning [as well as] my abdomen and my upper body. The stationary bicycle I do every day now at my doctor's suggestion because of a knee injury." Jon has race-walked more than 30 marathons, along with innumerable shorter-distance races, "I always do the San Francisco Half Marathon and lots of 20-kilometer race-walks," he says. "I work out about three times a week to maintain my physical condition until my knee gets back in operation."

Steve Scott says, "One morning I walk; another I'm on the stationary bike." He also exercises in his pool—"sort of swimming, stretching, and swimming again. This pool's not big enough to swim in, but I play in it, do water therapy. Walking in water is good for you."

"A real gym rat" is how Will Belais describes himself. "I go to the gym every day. In my early 60s there was real progress." Since then, though, he feels his "body has changed dramatically. I started to thicken out again, and I can't get back down."

Mike is up at 5 o'clock every day for at-home exercising. "It's all [done according to] a little book that tells me how many times to run in place. Then I do push-ups and sit-ups and lift weights." And this hour-plus workout is only the preamble to his beach walk. "I walk eight to 10 miles a day, roughly five miles each way from where I live to the beach, seven days a week year-round. In the winter I do it even when the weather's bad. I've been know to walk along the beach with an umbrella while it's raining. I walk a lot."

Perhaps the most avid exerciser, though, is runner Tom Pait, who has completed more than 60 marathons, including the 1990 and 1994 Gay Games Marathon. "I get up in the morning, stretch, and then run to the Golden Gate Bridge, a six- or eight-miler." He says he is less focused on competing than he used to be. "Now, I just run for myself. I'm not training for anything."

Walking, running, swimming, and working out at the gym are popular among the men interviewed but far from the only physical activities they engage in. Norm Self does a 20-minute yoga routine "very religiously every day." Robert Bettinger says, "I get physical exercise clearing paths and doing work around the lagoon where I live. I do yoga, walk a lot, and swim." He also enjoys kayaking and hiking, and each year he spends "10 days in the Montana mountains, hiking, and backpacking."

Not everyone, though, is an exercise enthusiast. Ed Conlon says, "I avoid as much exercise as possible, because it's boring. In my living room I have a stationary bicycle, and I'll ride five to 10 miles as I watch television. Without the TV, I don't think I would climb on that bike just to peddle and look at four walls."

George Casper used to enjoy all types of exercise. "Exercise through my life was strenuous in the out-of-doors: rock climbing, spelunking, whitewater canoeing, and mountain biking." But back surgery at 45 limited George's physical activities. "I'm much more severely restricted in what I can do now," he says.

The men who still work full-time are limited by lack of time. Still, though, they manage to exercise. For farmer Rod Harrington, "It's primarily walking, climbing into grain bins, climbing into the tractor, doing mechanical work on tractors and machines." Charles claims that even his Wall Street job provides exercise: "My doctor says going up and down stairs 20 to 30 times a day is exercise."

BAD HABITS

"I smoked for about a year as a young man, until I walked up my first mountain in New England and saw what it was doing to me."

—*George Casper*

Cigarettes, alcohol, and drugs are part of gay life, whether we like it or not. Studies have shown that gay men and lesbians are more likely to smoke cigarettes than their straight counterparts. An estimated 41% of gay men and lesbians in the United States smoke, as opposed to 27% of men and 22% of women in the general population (percentages that include the number of gay men and lesbians who smoke). Similarly skewed figures exist for the proportion of gay men and lesbians who regularly consume alcohol. Anecdotal evidence points to high rates of illegal drug use, though the men interviewed for this book do not bear this out, perhaps because drug use is less common for their generation than for those that followed.

Nearly all the men say they smoked at one time, but most quit years ago. Only a few continue to smoke. Tom Pait smoked for a few years but stopped around 1980 when he started running.

John Peters "smoked very heavily until about 1962. I quit when my son was born." George of New York City admits, "I smoked a pack and a half [a day] for 30 years," but he doesn't smoke now. Rod Harrington also used to smoke; he's stopped twice, the second time "about five years ago." Similarly, Ben Fowler says, "I stopped for about 14 years, then I started again in '80. I quit for good about five years ago." Ed Conlon stopped smoking at age 54 when he first took on his Queen Eddie persona. "I didn't think it [smoking] was ladylike, and I did not want to set an example of having a cigarette hanging out of my mouth and ashes falling."

The men who still smoke are Richard Malloy, who has smoked all his life, and Frank Poe. Fifteen years ago, Frank participated in a stop-smoking program and managed to curb his craving for cigarettes for about a year. "After I quit, there wasn't a day went by that I didn't want a cigarette," he says. "So I [thought that] when I get older, like I am now, what difference will it make whether I live another year or two years? That's my attitude." Frank's partner, Ed Wright, was a smoker as well. For the year that Frank went cold turkey, their relationship as a smoker and nonsmoker worked well. Ed "didn't smoke that much anyway and always went outside if he needed to take few puffs."

Alcohol consumption is more prevalent than smoking among the men interviewed. Many admit to current or past drinking problems, which they often overcame through either self-discipline or the help of Alcoholics Anonymous. All the men came of age in an era when drinking alcohol was readily accepted, even expected, in many social contexts. Several interviewees who feel they have no drinking problem nevertheless qualify as social drinkers by contemporary standards. Ed Conlon is typical. "I drank quite a bit, but it was never a problem. I drank to socialize. I would not classify myself as an alcoholic, but I did drink quite a bit and that included at least two cocktails before dinner every night until the time of cancer."

Quite a few of the men have learned to restrict their alcohol intake or have quit drinking entirely. George of New York City curtailed his drinking for health reasons. "After this last illness, I just stopped drinking." He admits he drank excessively for much of his life. "People around me were heavy drinkers," he says. "I myself was not a particularly happy heavy drinker, so I stopped drinking." Since undergoing heart surgery, Jim Edmonds has limited his alcohol intake on doctor's orders: "One glass of wine a day with dinner and that's it." Likewise, John Peters concedes, "I used to be able to drink a 24-beer pack like nothing before my stroke. But boy, I don't do that anymore." For José Sarría, the turning point was a bout with hepatitis 40 years ago. His doctor told him his liver would be ruined if he continued drinking. Now José seldom drinks hard liquor. "It has to be a special occasion," he says. "I occasionally have wine with dinner."

Milton Lestz, Robert of Palm Desert, and Robert Tingling all claim they "never" or "only rarely" drink alcohol. Bill Worrall says, "I've never been drunk once in my life. I'll have maybe a glass of wine if people are over for dinner or if I go out." Lee Denman likes wine with his meals but feels he never has had a drinking problem. He will "have one or two drinks at the most" whenever he's at the Capri Lounge, his nephew's gay bar in Oceanside, Calif. That Lee is the Capri's treasurer does not tempt him to drink more. He recollects that "the bar was prohibited from having dancing or live music when it originated almost 20 years ago." The Capri became Oceanside's "first legal establishment to offer [alcohol along with] live entertainment and dancing."

Several of the men feel that they may have had or could have easily developed a drinking problem. George Casper says, "I am one of those people who could easily have a drinking problem." Consequently, he has learned to monitor his drinking closely. "I'm always very, very aware of how much I'm drinking and when and why." Jon Borset thinks he may have had a drinking problem but resolved it just with "will power." Similarly, Will Belais feels alcohol could have become a problem for him if he hadn't simply "decided not to drink." In addition to a stop-smoking program, Frank Poe also went through a stop-drinking program and feels he "got rid of" a potential problem. "I didn't drink any alcohol for about a year or two," he says. "Now, maybe I have two drinks a week." Tom Pait, who still usually has a beer on Sunday night, says, "Yeah, I kinda had a drinking problem, more or less. Sometimes, if I go to hear jazz in a club, I'll have more beers than I can hold and get a little dizzy. I don't fall down or anything. I could go on drinking beer all night, but I don't." Fred thinks he may have had a problem too. "Long ago, when I was working, I was a heavy social drinker," he says. "I understand how people become alcoholics."

"That monkey I carried for 20 years" is how Norm Self describes his alcohol problem. "I was a closeted drunk as well as a closeted gay. I don't know if there's a connection, but I had 'em both." He recalls that by 1989 "there were signs of the demon growing. A year before, I had made kind of a blood oath with my wife that I would quit and never drink again, and if I ever did drink again, I'd go to rehab willingly. My blood oath only lasted a year." He adds, "Alcohol was going to kill me, but it hadn't reached the phys-iological stage yet. Spiritually, I was at risk of death. It was only a matter of time until my body would be gone too. Yeah, I think it all [would have come] crashing in at once." Norm now views becoming sober as "one of the most important things in my life, like dropping a millstone that I was carrying."

Steve Scott curtailed his drinking by joining AA. "I'll have 30 years next April without drinking at all," he says. "I'm not that active in AA now. Occasionally I'll go to a meeting." But regarding the impact AA made on him, he avows, "It saved my life."

John Schiappi's story is perhaps the most dramatic of the men interviewed. "I started drinking when I was age 17 and was an alcoholic right from the start." Unfortunately, he didn't "recognize it and certainly didn't really deal with it" until reaching the age of 49. Over his 32 years of active drinking, John spent six or seven nights in jail, was kicked out of law school, and totaled a car. Still, he functioned "well and ably" in a working environment. The year 1977 brought about "a six-month turning point." John's wife had started going to AA, and his 19-year-old son had been experiencing "problems with alcohol and drugs and had to go into a mental institution in order to keep out of jail." At the same time, John was coming to terms with being gay while still drinking heavily himself. After working through some issues in therapy, John came out to his wife, and they separated. "I had always thought that I drank because I had an alcoholic wife and a drug-addicted son," he notes. But he learned to acknowledge that he was chemically dependent too. "Living by myself, I was still drinking heavily. I knew enough about AA by that time that I just started going to meetings. Blessedly, I've been sober ever since." He adds, "The openness and sharing from AA is probably one of the most important lessons in my life: learning that the more openly you share your vulnerability and anxieties, the more likely you are to strengthen rather than weaken friendships." As an example, John says, "My wife ended up dying of throat cancer. In a six-month period she died and my son got sober." He and his wife never divorced. "We actually became reconciled during her terminal illness. In fact, I was the only one she would permit to visit her at the hospital."

Perhaps reflecting their generation's social habits, nearly all the men report they have never used recreational drugs. One man, Ed Conlon, asks, "What are recreational drugs?" Frank Poe swears, "No, no drugs ever. No drugs, period." Ben Fowler gives a similar response: "No. Absolutely no drugs, no marijuana, no hard drugs— I'm dead set against them." And perhaps for good measure, Ben is "dead set against gambling too."

Jim Mitchell, however, admits, "I smoked marijuana briefly in the early '70s. I found I didn't like it. It put me to sleep all the time, so I quit, and I've never used anything else. No hard drugs."

Only one of the men admitted to using hard drugs, although he declined to be identified as a drug user. "I've been a user of cocaine for 20 years, but I find that now I'm going months without using it anymore. Friends of mine can look at a peanut and immediately get addicted to peanuts. I can snort coke and walk away from it. Same with liquor. Same with cigarettes."

INJURY AND ILLNESS

"I really haven't had any sickness—a couple of running injuries, but I've gotten them taken care of."
—*Tom Pait*

Remaining healthy is a priority for all the men interviewed. However, it is impossible to go through life without accumulating a few bumps and bruises along the way. Most of the men, though, even those with serious illnesses or injuries, continue to live normal and independent lives. Ed Conlon, for instance, considers his health good, though he admits "that may sound strange from someone with cancer." José Sarría says, "I had asthma as a child. After working so many years in smoky bars, asthma came back very badly." He cites a California law that bans smoking in all bars and restaurants as very important to his health. "I don't have any problem [with asthma] now. I have a little arthritis, but I swim and that's helping a lot."

Even men who have been severely incapacitated by illness or a debilitating injury remain upbeat about their health. Bob suffered a crushed arm at age 3. "I'm handicapped," he says, "and that has prevented me from taking part in a lot of activities." But his crushed arm has not stopped him from becoming an avid skier, a strenuous hiker, or from designing, cutting, and maintaining hiking trails.

George Casper has been a paraplegic twice in his life. In both instances his condition "was not correctable except by surgery, the last time by very major surgery." He adds, "So I'm lucky to be able to walk…. I can't lift things; I can't shovel snow or push automobiles, but I have mobility. I can get around. I carry a cane when I travel."

Ed of Oakland has had a few brushes with physical impairment too. "I was in the South Pacific for five years during the war, and I developed arthritis," he states. "And I had problems with my right hip. I waited and waited and waited, and finally I had it [replaced] with a new hip 18 months ago. I walked with a cane for a while, then walked around the lake, and gradually I gave the cane up." John Kiley has also had a hip replacement. He cites arthritis as "a bit of a problem, but things are working well."

Norm Self recalls two significant hospital stays, the first at age 9 for a ruptured appendix. "I nearly died. If it hadn't been for sulfa—penicillin didn't exist then—I would've died. I've still got the scar. The other really significant hospitalization was a turning point and great crossroads for me, when I spent a month in alcoholic rehabilitation 10 years ago. It turned my life around."

George of New York City sounds almost baffled that he's lived as long as he has. "I have the idea that I was not really meant to be, that I should have been a statistic, but I survived. An awful lot of peripheral systems have gone badly for me. I've had a number of serious illnesses in my life and survived every one, but at the cost of a certain amount of stamina." He cites one episode as "life-threatening and mysterious" in the extreme. "I suddenly felt dreadfully, terribly ill, couldn't understand why, and neither could the doctors. Four o'clock in the morning in the emergency room, only to discover that I have a high coagulation [rate]. That's the opposite of the people whose blood doesn't clot. Mine clots too rapidly." After corrective surgery to remove a portion of his small intestine, George has returned to health.

Steve Scott has also had some strange medical experiences. "I've had back surgery and surgery that no one on earth except my doctors ever heard of. That involved the removal of skin and scar tissue caused by a shingles attack." He still experiences residual pain, but "it's getting better."

Heart conditions affect many of the men. Bill Strong says, "I've had four heart attacks. One time I had an angioplasty; another time we just let nature take its course, let another valve open up. The last time, two years ago while on vacation, I had a heart attack that ended in a four-way bypass."

Lee Denman says, "Over the years, I've had quite a few surgeries, including a tumor removed from my heart. I drove myself to work seven days after that surgery, and I recovered pretty well. Four years ago, I had congestive heart failure. The doctor told me I could drop dead today, tomorrow, next week, next month. I didn't care for that attitude so I changed doctors and medication. Last January the doctor told me my heart had returned to normal functioning."

Jim Edmonds reports that he had double-bypass surgery nearly 15 years ago and more recently an angioplasty. More than a dozen years ago, Richard Malloy had an aorta transplant. Frank Poe underwent bypass surgery about 20 years ago and says, "I was knocked off my pins for about a year before I got over that." Jim of Michigan had three-way bypass surgery about a year ago And both Milton Lestz and Clee live comfortably with pacemakers.

"Ten years ago, I had a stroke, which was really debilitating," says John Peters. "With therapy I learned to walk and to talk again. But I didn't stick with therapy and relearn how to write, so I can't write today. I can sign my name, but beyond that I don't write so anybody can read it. I'm left-handed, and I can't use that hand at all. I tried writing with my right hand, but I lost patience."

Ed Conlon relates, ""Two and a half years ago, I was diagnosed with cancer in my head and neck, and I'm being treated for that. It's a roller-coaster ride. You never know when you're going to have a setback because of side effects. I've been able to live with it extremely well and accept it very well."

A year ago, Norman Eckelberger was diagnosed with prostate cancer. "They caught it within months," he says, quite relieved. "I was being checked every six months, and when I had the routine check and cancer was discovered, it had been just matter of a few months. I went through radiation—a radioactive seed implant to kill the cancer. It was a real breeze. There was nothing to it. Now I have a checkup every six months. I've been just fine." John Schiappi also was diagnosed with prostate cancer and says, "The prostate cancer certainly heads the list with a hospital stay and surgery." He adds, "For the past couple of years I've had a bout with bizarre insomnia that seems related to environmental factors in my home, but that seems to now be under control."

Will Belais remained hospital-free until a series of maladies hit him. "All of a sudden I was in the hospital quite a bit. I had pneumonia in '89, which was a shock, and I thought it was AIDS, but it turned out to be bacterial pneumonia—had to do with air-conditioning. I had two hernia operations within a week of each other. I had a penile implant that did not work well and had it done again. Very traumatic. From that point on, there's been some deterioration in my health, and I'm not very happy about that." Will has seen both a psychologist and a psychiatrist in the past but had to discontinue sessions because of insurance payment problems. "I have emotional problems that center on two things: I'm not a good money manager, and I feel extremely lonely. I have felt lonely for a very long time, even though I'm around people a lot. I'm quite convinced it's my age."

Many of the men report having had sexually transmitted diseases such as urethritis and gonorrhea. Other STDs the men have contracted include syphilis, genital herpes, and anal warts. Some had contracted STDs while enlisted in the U.S. Armed Services during World War II or the Korean War. The men report that the STDs they've had were transmitted just as often through heterosexual sex as homosexual sex. One man, who prefers not to be named in this context, recalls how he contracted venereal disease when he first joined the army during World War II: "I think it was [from] heterosexual contact. I'd only been with women three times in my life, and I think it was the second time."

Several of the men report no history of STDs. One attributes his STD-free status to the fact that "sex has been very unimportant in my life." Another man says, "My only close experience was coming home once and finding somebody else had used the bed. I didn't know [about that], and I got a bad case of crabs."

One man has had repeated bouts of STDs. "From the '50s through the '70s, I got my share of gonorrhea, probably three or four times, and I got syphilis once. Since the early '80s, I haven't had any sexually transmitted diseases."

HIV/AIDS is an unavoidable concern for gay men of any age, though none of the men interviewed express an inordinate amount of anxiety about it. Most have been tested for HIV and know their status to be negative. None report they are HIV-positive.

Jim Mitchell, however, had a close call. "I was diagnosed with Kaposi's sarcoma, even though I'm HIV-negative. In fact, I was falsely diagnosed as having AIDS in 1986. Only after extensive testing did they determine I did not have AIDS." As a result, he says, "I [have been in studies] at Columbia Presbyterian Hospital and at the Aaron Diamond Institute, both in New York City. Aaron Diamond is using my blood to try to develop an antibody to the KS virus. The study at Columbia used my blood to identify that virus."

Knowing their HIV status is important to most of the men. Among the several who monitor their HIV status regularly, one man reports, "I get tested for HIV regularly, probably a couple times a year, even though I think I play safe. Sometime between the time I go to get the blood drawn and go back for the results, I think, 'Oh my God, what if...' Even with those little moments of 'what ifs' I'm not traumatized or worried. It's more of a routine thing."

Paying for Health care

"I know health care coverage is a sinister problem in our society, but it's one that hasn't hit me yet because I'm so healthy. I'm not worried about it yet, but I know that it's out there as a potential problem."

—*Norm Self*

Though many of the men interviewed say they worry about their ability to pay for health care, few would count themselves among the 40% of Americans who have no health insurance. HMOs such as Kaiser Permanente Senior Advantage and Blue Cross and Blue Shield cover health care for most of the men. Also, several men have supplemental long-term care programs. A few have gone so far as to designate someone with power of attorney to make health care decisions for them if they are ever incapacitated. Those who remain in the work force have a combination of employer-provided and supplementary health care coverage.

John Schiappi feels fortunate because his former employer, the Bureau of National Affairs, is an "employee-owned organization" that is "very liberal with employee benefits." John says BNA is one of the increasingly rare companies that extends health insurance to retirees. "My primary coverage is Medicare but backed up with BNA insurance, which is particularly good because it covers prescription medications." John has designated power of attorney for health care to "a very good gay friend" he had hired at BNA: "a skilled executive assistant, the ideal person [to be] the executor on my will."

Lifetime-care facility resident Ed of Oakland doesn't worry about health care costs for himself or his partner, Bob. "Buy into a lifetime-care facility and you're taken over by them. You turn your Medicare over to them. The foundation will pay."

Veterans benefits provide comprehensive health care for those men who've seen military service. Robert Bettinger says, "Right now, my health care costs are handled. I'm with VA health care, and a Veterans hospital would probably help with most everything else." Mike says, "I'm in Senior Prime Time with the Navy. I could have joined other things, but I said no because the Navy always takes care of me." Bill Strong says he goes "mainly through the VA," for health care. "So long as I've got the VA, that's fine."

Feelings about HMOs are mixed. Jon Borset says, "It's wonderful at Kaiser Senior Advantage because you don't have any major expenses." Bud Jordan praises his HMO for how it covered a leg operation, first for $33,000 and then a follow-up operation for $20,000. He says, "Well, they talk about HMOs, but I never had [to pay] one penny out of my pocket for the leg operations. They never sent me one bill. Not one penny did I pay."

Will Belais, however, is less happy. Will continues to work, and his job provides coverage through Blue Cross and Blue Shield, which he despises. "They keep insisting that I'm eligible for Medicare, but I don't want it. I'm fully employed and feel I don't need it. My employers and I pay for health insurance, but Blue Cross/Blue Shield won't pay my claims. I'm very angry about it. My budget is thin, and if health care becomes a major issue, I'm bankrupt."

While satisfied with his HMO coverage, José Sarría is concerned about how others fare. "I don't know how some people manage. I really, truly don't." José has managed to put away a "little money" and has health insurance coverage, so he feels he will "always be able to handle health problems." He also has designated a power of attorney for health care decisions, including whether or not to continue life support in case of terminal illness. "I've been a very firm believer in having that organized from year one. I was brought up that when members of my family die, all we have to do is mourn, because everything else is all taken care of ahead of time."

CHAPTER 5
Homes and Cars

WHERE WE LIVE

"As long as I can live in my own house, I will."
—Lee Denman

The 41 men interviewed for this book live in a variety of settings and a broad spectrum of locations, ranging from New York City to a Missouri farm to retirement communities around the country. For the most part, they still live in private homes, town houses, or apartments. Owners and renters are represented in nearly equal numbers. In New York and Los Angeles, gay men often live alone, which is typical for those cities. In January 2001, *The New York Times* reported that although "two thirds of people over 65 in the United States live with a spouse of relative...studies in New York and Los Angeles have found that 65% to 75% of elderly gay people live alone."

A recent phenomenon is the development of gay retirement communities. One is already in operation: Palms of Manasota in Palmetto, Fla. The California-based Lundberg Group is planning another: Our Town. The group's founder, Peter Lundberg, has a list of 1,700 people who have expressed an interest in living in a gay and lesbian retirement community. "We are raising equity money and expect to break ground in 2005," he says. Similar planned communities are being proposed for Boston, Fort Lauderdale, and Santa Fe, N.M.

Not everyone, however, is rushing to live in a gay retirement community. New York's Senior Pride Network reports "no universal need or desire to march en masse into 'defined communities.'" The organization maintains, "If there were clean and simple answers, housing developers would have identified them and secured funding. Most seniors 'age in place.' They grow older and die in an environment where they spent most of their years, in a familiar... community."

"Aging in place" seems most likely for the men who live in their own house or condominium. Charles lives in the same house he has owned for 32 years and plans to continue living there "until death takes me out." He describes his home and the community of 43,000 people in which he lives: "My house is 90-some years old, but most are 60- or 70-year-old houses—nice trees on the street, well-kept lawns. I like where I live."

Jack and his partner, Bob, are equally enthusiastic about their home. Together they own a waterfront town house in Wilton Manors, Fla., an enclave completely surrounded by Fort Lauderdale. "We have a gay mayor and two gay council members," Jack says. "I'd say between 40% and 50% of Wilton Manors is gay. We love it here. It's beautiful, safe, convenient to everything—simply wonderful. And we plan to stay here."

Since the mid 1950s, Fred and Clee have owned their San Francisco home with its drop-dead view of the city and the bay. They love the house and plan to stay there. Fred says, "This is the only place I want to live. We keep in mind we're never going to move. It's paid for. We will make every effort to stay here, including [arranging for] somebody coming in to help." The couple describes their neighborhood as "definitely mixed. Most of our neighbors, up until this past year, had lived here from 40 to 50 years." The men have experienced few problems with their neighbors. Clee says, "We fit into the community. There are straights with babies raised next door, and so forth. In fact, we hosted a 'gay baby shower' for the woman next door. It was a riot."

Mel Clark lives with his partner of 17 years in the house they own in Annapolis, Md. "We could retire easily now, sell and move where the cost of living is lower, but we like this area very much, and we want to stay." Several years ago, Mel and his partner realized that the burden of home ownership was becoming too heavy for them, but they came up with a solution. "We took in a friend five or six years ago who was out of work. He does the cooking, gardening, and stuff like that. Now in his mid 30s, he's working but still does what cooking he can. He sort of became a surrogate son to us."

After globe-hopping through 27 countries while living abroad, Lee Denman calls his Oceanside, Calif., neighborhood "one of the nicest areas I've lived in" and adds, "I like living near the beach." Lee has owned the house he lives in now for four years but has resided on the same street for almost 15. "We've rented two houses on this street at different times, and when this house became available to purchase, we bought it, because I don't like improving rental property." He lives in the house with his brother, his nephew, and a student from Mexico. When asked about his favorite spots overseas, Lee says, "Of the 27 countries I've lived in, probably the most pleasant was Singapore." He says it's the only place he has ever found that he likes more than Oceanside.

John Schiappi is a 35-year homeowner living in the northwest section of Washington, D.C. He describes his community as "country living in the city: somewhat suburban, but with a very neighborly feel to it." John lives alone and says he is "very happy" with where he's at now, but adds, "At some point, I might consider apartment living."

Both Jim Edmonds and Bill Strong own homes in university towns—Jim in Cheney, Wash.; Bill in Sewanee, Tenn. Jim has owned his house since 1976 and shares it with his three sisters. "Cheney is a university town, so it's very liberal," he says. Likewise, Bill characterizes Sewanee as "very open, very understanding" and attributes the enlightened atmosphere to the overriding community presence of the University of the South. Both men are pleased that their communities are so accepting, and they plan to stay put.

Norm Self owns his home but says he might move if he met someone. "If I met somebody and we agreed to live together, my bias would be toward finding a third place—neither him coming to mine or me going to his. But I'm happy where I am. I can see myself living here the rest of my life."

Not everyone, though, is happy with where they live, even if they remain adamant about owning their own home. José Sarría says, "I've always lived in a house. I want a back door and a front door." He now lives in a rural community in northern California that he describes as "very small, straight, and poor." That milieu is very frustrating for José. "Here, I am more or less a prisoner. It's 130 miles to go into San Francisco and costs an arm and a leg." However, José is planning a move to Palm Springs, about which he is very excited. "I'll be right in the middle of a very social community. I can go to the corner, take a bus, or hop on a golf cart and ride around."

Dave and his partner own a home in a Tamarac, Fla., retirement community for people age 50 and older, but they are considering moving because of "nosy neighbors." Dave likes the idea of living in a gay and lesbian retirement community.

In contrast with Dave, Richard Malloy and his partner, Tucker, cite just the opposite problem. Richard lambastes the "shitty" Washington, D.C., suburb where they reside: "[It's] the only place we've ever lived where we don't have [friendly] neighbors. First, we saw that as homophobic, but it wasn't that at all. Nobody that has ever lived here—in a 30-house area—has ever spoken [to their neighbors]. It's a very transient D.C. area, not at all like when we had our 50th anniversary and neighbors came to visit along with their families, their grandchildren, and everybody else." Richard is unsure whether he and Tucker will stay in their current residence.

Jim Mitchell owns a home in a community he describes as "originally a weekend summer resort" that has since grown into a year-round area. He lives alone now but thinks he may "need to get into an apartment because of health condition." He explains, "I live on the side of a hill. The couple of times I've had to call 911 to take an ambulance, it was very difficult to manage the hill."

Owning a condominium or apartment can eliminate much of the hassle of home ownership, though other problems often crop up. Will Belais, for instance, lives in a northwest Washington, D.C., condo development that he estimates is 80% gay, a large reason why he chose that particular complex. "Those of us who are gay tend to congregate. When you go down the main street of this community, it's essentially gay men." However, living in the condo development has some drawbacks. "A lot of rules here I didn't expect—rules that have nothing to do with being gay, just rules," Will states. "When I moved in, I didn't know what the rules really were, and I broke them all very quickly. I was told that I had two parking spaces. One day there was no place to park, so I just parked my car and complained about somebody taking my space. I was told I had a right to enter and park, but no reserved space, which seemed to me like paying this huge fee for a hunting license." Another problem arose when the trucks delivering his furniture were too large. "I didn't know there was a rule about truck size, over which I had no control." Will has worked through his frustrations, though, and plans to stay where he is.

Robert Tingling likes living in his condominium in Coral Springs, Fla., which describes as a "working-class community." He moved there from Phoenix after his partner died. "I had no other choice," he says. "I had to move because I couldn't keep the house [in Phoenix]. My niece, who is a nurse and lives here, invited me to come here so that she could be nearer to me."

For 10 years Ben Fowler has owned a town house in a San Diego condo complex that he describes as "basically a retired community." He considers where he lives as "the finest [place] in the United States—convenient to the interstate and close to the ocean." Ben plans to stay put with his partner, Lee, although he may install a chair elevator on account of the town house's two stories.

New York City apartment owner, George, feels good about the Upper West Side Manhattan apartment he has owned and lived in for about 25 years. "My congressman, Gerry Nadler, lives on the third floor. Cecily Tyson lives upstairs." George believes he's made a sound real estate investment. "[I] bought astutely. I am amazed at how smart I was in those days, that the person who lived then in my skin was a very smart person. Twenty-five years ago, I bought this place at the bottom of a market for $25,000 or $26,000. It's now worth about $350,000." He has no plans to move. "My only way of turning my earlier stroke of astuteness into cash is to sell the apartment, but then I'd have to move someplace, so the dilemma presents itself."

The men who rent housing are generally happy with where they live. John Peters rents half of a duplex in a small eastern Iowa town. "We're just off the Mississippi River with Illinois on one side of the river, Iowa on the other," he explains. He's been in his duplex for more than a decade and says he "would hate to move." But even though John "loves it" where he lives, he doubts he will stay for financial reasons. "Across the river my pension would not be taxed. It would save me several thousand dollars a year to live there."

Ed Conlon loves San Diego's gay-friendly North Park neighborhood, where he shares a sunny second-story two-bedroom apartment with his partner, Shawne. "It's very nice: wide, sunny streets; not overridden with crime—although I would not feel safe here to go out at night by myself. I think that's difficult to do in any city anymore." Despite his reservations about safety, Ed says, "I am very comfortable with our apartment."

Close friends Jon Borset and Tom Pait live near each other in San Francisco in rent-controlled apartments. Jon has lived in his apartment for "35, 38 years, something like that." He is "very happy" and plans to stay there. "The house I live in is all Asian-American— always has been—and is owned by an Asian man, and everyone speaks [East] Asian languages except me. So I don't have much contact with the people, although they're very friendly. Most of them don't speak English." On nearby Polk Street, Tom Pait has been in his apartment for 35 years. Tom rents a room to a friend to help with the bills. "I'd love to stay here for the rest of my life," he says.

Rod Harrington bought a manufactured home to economize since his divorce was expensive, but he plans to live in it temporarily.

"I have bought my parents' traditional house from my nieces," he explains. Rod plans to remodel his parents' former home, which is about a mile from where he temporarily resides, and move into it in two or three years.

Another manufactured-home resident, Steve Scott, enjoys living in a Palm Desert mobile home park limited to people 55 and older. With a spacious living room overlooking a cactus garden and a pool, Steve's home is hardly wanting for comfort—never mind pop culture's low-end image of trailer parks. Steve boasts, "This is a mobile home park—a big one, probably the best in the desert." Steve has lived there for nearly a decade, and Norman Eckelberger spends several days there every week with him. Steve considers Norman "more than a friend; this is a relationship."

When Norman is not with Steve, he lives with Bud Jordan in Palm Springs in a manufactured home they have owned for the past six years. Bud and Norman's home is also in a self-contained community limited to people 55 and older. Bud enthuses, "I love the gay life in Palm Springs and never in my life thought I'd live in a place like this, where you're accepted as you are." Norman likes living with Bud. "It's never been a sexual thing," he admits. "I'm there with Bud three days a week, and at Steve's house four days a week." Norman tries to reserve Thursdays, Fridays, and Saturdays for staying with Steve, while the other days are for Bud. "But it can vary a little bit, depending upon the circumstances," Norman says. "It's a different kind of situation, I suppose, from what most people do, but it works out for me beautifully. I like it."

Bill Worrall, who still works full-time, owns a "triple-wide manufactured home in a country-club community" in Palm Desert but is looking into other living options. "Somebody wants me to come to Australia; another wants me to come to Brazil. I don't know what I'll do. I could live here the rest of my life. I've just started to think about what I want to do when I stop working." Bill is nevertheless "OK" with where and how he lives now. "I lived in a really expensive house when my partner was alive, but when he died, I couldn't handle it by myself, so now I'm into something that I can afford." Affordability is also a concern for Cyprian Fary, who lives in a manufactured home in nearby Thousand Palms. "It's OK," he says. "I can afford it."

Robert Bettinger describes his accommodations as a trailer, not a mobile home. "A trailer is under 400 square feet: That's the distinction." He owns the trailer and lives with his partner on an 800-acre nature preserve in San Diego County, Calif. "I'm so happy with where I live and how I live that I don't want to change it."

Ed of Oakland and his partner, Bob, are the only interviewees who reside in a lifetime-care facility. Ed says Bob and he are pleased with their living arrangement at St. Paul's Towers, although Ed admits he gets mad sometimes, "because I can't run the place." He explains, "When we had our own home, we could do what we wanted to do. Here we have to deal with a structure that is a little rigid at times." Ed is upbeat, though, about the kind of treatment Bob and he have received as a gay couple. "People know we're gay. We're probably the first two males who openly came out when we moved here. And we came in with that clarity with the management on the issue of being gay. We were the first; we broke the barrier. I like to feel we created the image that it is possible to do this. We have a good number of friends who have moved into San Francisco Towers, our sister facility, who are living a very happy life there." When presented with the idea of living in an all-gay retirement community, Ed says he prefers his current setup.

Jim Mitchell is "thinking about" living in an all-gay retirement facility. "I investigated one down in Florida," he says. "I've forgotten its name, but at the time I investigated, I thought the two guys who were running it were very unrealistic, so I rejected it. Things have changed since then, but I'm not sure I want to live in Florida. The only part of Florida I sort of like is the Keys, but I don't know of any gay retirement options there."

Overall, the men vary widely in reaction to the idea of living in an all-gay retirement community. Will Belais likes the idea of living where "at least we can talk about things." Richard Malloy says, "If I was younger I would establish one—begin it. The money is there. It's needed, very essentially needed, particularly for people who are alone or for couples." Norm Self states, "I have no problem living in a gay place, but…I have no desire to live in a retirement home of any stripe or denomination. But if I were going to, I'd love for it to be gay." Conversely, Jim Edmonds asserts, "I don't think I would enjoy it." John Peters also feels "very little desire to live that way," and Milton Lestz says he doesn't think retiring to an all-gay environment "would suit my needs."

AUTOMOBILES AND DRIVING

"I have never driven in my life. Born and raised as I was in New York City, it was much easier to put a nickel in the subway to get where you were going."
—*Ed Conlon*

The American Dream used to mean a car in every garage. True to that image, most of the 41 men interviewed own and operate an automobile. Several men have two vehicles. A few, though, do not own cars or have limited driving experience or, like Ed Conlon, do not drive at all.

Mike says he has never had a driver's license. "The only time I drove …[was while] I was being taught how. I was in the Navy and about 26. My friend says he's going to teach me how to drive. I had been drinking a little bit. So we go out to the golf course in Memphis in a big old 6-by-6 truck. Naturally, I drove onto the golf course, and I ruined it. After that experience, I said, 'No, I'll never get a license.'" Likewise, Bob says he "never learned" how to drive. He lives in an Arizona community where, in the absence of extensive public transportation, it is very important for him to be situated conveniently to stores and any services he might need.

Many of the men have curtailed the amount of driving they do as they've grown older. Robert Tingling "used to drive" but does not own a car now. Ed of Oakland owns a car, but drives "as little as I can." Fred and Clee also own a car but seldom drive it.

CHAPTER 6

Women, Families of Origin, Straights

MARRIAGE

"I was married to a lesbian once. She was in the service and needed to look like she was... straight."

—*Tom Pait*

The 41 men came of age in a time when young men were expected to marry women, no matter what. And many gay men did just that. Surprisingly, though, nearly half of the men interviewed never married. Two report that they were engaged but broke things off before actually tying the knot. One man is still officially married to his wife. A second, Tom Pait, may be since he has not seen the woman he married years ago and never divorced.

A few men say that from the very beginning their wives knew they were gay. George Casper, who married at age 22, says about his former spouse, "She knew I was gay from my lips, and from my college roommate who had told her the same thing in case I hadn't." George and his wife stayed married for 23 years before obtaining a divorce 25 years ago. "My wife decided that she did not want to be married to me any longer." George cites "the gay stuff" as one of the grounds for their divorce.

Mel Clark, who married at 21, says, "We were in college in Columbia, Mo., living in married student housing. There was a guy upstairs who was taking my same curriculum. His wife worked nights. I studied with him, and we carried on. My wife knew about that." As to the rationale behind this arrangement, Mel reflects, "I got married because I didn't want to hurt her feelings by breaking off the relationship. Marrying ended up hurting her more." He and his wife stayed married for 16 years, an experience he describes as "sort of like living with your sister." Mel says that he had sex with men during his marriage. Of his eventual breakup with his wife, he says, "I finally got to thinking: Our kids are growing up. In another 10 years they will be gone. I'm going to come home and sit at the dining room table and talk to her. I want out."

John Schiappi says, "Once, when I was on probation from having been arrested yet again for alcoholic gay sexual behavior, I was assigned to see a therapist who tried to convince me that I could overcome my gay tendencies through heterosexual activity. I tried with my then wife-to-be. She helped me to experiment with heterosexual sex with the result that she got pregnant and we married." John and his wife stayed married for 20 years and had two children together, though after two or three years of marriage he was back to having sex with men. "In the early years ours was a pretty good marriage. To this day I have not found anybody else I was as compatible with intellectually, spiritually, and in sharing activities. It was just that sexually we were not compatible."

Fred was married twice. His first wife did not know he was gay; however, "the second [wife], I told her." About his first wife he recollects: "The girl I married I knew in college back in Ohio. She came out here to San Francisco determined to get married. I was only 20. I had no idea what I was doing." He continues, "She was pretty sharp, worked in a department store, but stole money from the company five different times and went back to Ohio. I never saw her again." He says his second marriage was motivated by "peer pressure, family pressure." Neither marriage produced children.

Milton Lestz and Norm Self were also married twice. Milton was married for about a year each time, the first ending in an annulment, the second in divorce. Norm married for the first time at age 23. "I was married for 28 years: That's a long time. The second time, it lasted only four years." He describes his current relations with both ex-wives as "splendid." He adds, "I never had children with either woman, but my second wife has a daughter, and her children, whom I call my granddaughters, are very special in my life." Norm says of his first wife, "We've become more intimate in the last few months than when we were married. I see her a few times a year. We talk a lot on the phone; we're still very good buddies. When I came out to her, that intensified our closeness. When I got into this first gay love affair and shared that with her, she opened up in ways we never knew when we were married. The intimacy has just intensified."

Jim Edmonds says his marriage came about because he had an extra concert ticket. "We started dating by accident when she was a student. I had an extra ticket for a concert. I knocked on some dorm doors and asked if anyone wanted to go, and she said yes. 'It means going with me,' I replied, and she accepted. That started our dating." The marriage was childless and ended in 1974. The reason for the divorce was "just incompatibility." Jim notes, "The lawyer said it was the friendliest case he'd ever handled." Jim admits that at first he was a little hesitant to finalize his divorce. "People [of my generation] just didn't divorce," he explains, adding, "I think we'd reached a point where we realized we were not going to be happy together, and there was no point in being miserable just to stay together. The one thing I don't know is if she knew I was gay."

John Peters says of his deceased wife, "I was married to a wonderful woman for only 11 years when she passed on. My son was only 9. I had a very happy marriage. If I could find another woman as good as her, I'd get married again. I'm not particularly looking, but if the right one came along, I would." When asked if he considers himself bisexual, John says, "Yes, I would say so." However, he hasn't had sex with a woman since his wife died. Similarly, he'd had sex with men before he married but not during his married years.

Dave married at 21 and fathered four children. While still married, he met his future life partner—then also married with children—in a hotel men's room. The men soon introduced their wives and families to one another, and the group began socializing and vacationing together. Meanwhile, the two fathers continued their romantic and sexual relationship. After the death of his wife, Dave's partner moved into Dave's household. They all lived together until Dave and his wife divorced. Now Dave and his partner live in a South Florida retirement community.

Will Belais says he is actually still married. "Legally, yes, we're married but separated. We went to a lawyer, did the whole nine yards, but we've not gone to court yet." Will recalls his early gay experiences: "I've had sexual encounters with men ever since I can remember, high school and college mates, mainly. When I met my wife, I responded to her emotionally." But Will had never had sex with a woman and was at a loss. "We get married. We're in the hotel room: I'm supposed to have intercourse with her, and I didn't know what to do. When it actually occurred, I was waiting for the bells and whistles. I was very disappointed." Despite this unspectacular show of passion, his wife got pregnant on their honeymoon. "We had our first baby very quickly, and another baby right away, two years and two weeks after the first one." Will says he never had sex with other women and that he tried "desperately to really be faithful, to honor my marriage vows." Yet after the birth of their second child he "started to go to gyms again and meet men in steam rooms." He told his wife he was gay. "That's been part of the problem," he says. His children also know. "My son had the toughest time with my being gay. My daughter doesn't make a big noise about it. I'm her dad— that's the end of it. My son and I have talked about it to the point that we're not talking to each other now."

Robert Bettinger didn't realize he was gay until after he'd married and started raising a family. "I married before I was aware that I was gay, and discovered after my four children were born that I was gay. That created tension, but I wanted to raise the children, so I stayed in the marriage for another 10 years, then felt it wasn't working and left the marriage." Finally, after 19 years he filed for divorce. Today, he continues to have a relationship with his children but not his ex-wife. He also has three grandchildren.

Bill Strong's story is similar. He was married for 29 years, fathered seven children, and raised a child "as my own" from his wife's previous marriage. He divorced "just before my youngest daughter's 17th birthday." Neither he nor his wife knew he was gay when they married, he says, but being gay was the reason for the divorce. Bill's children "certainly now know" he is gay, and proba- bly knew "at the time of the divorce too."

Mike married at age 41, just after he retired from the Navy. "I got out of the Navy in San Francisco, and this girl called—a WAVE I'd met while we were both stationed at the same base in Philadelphia. We got fond of each other—no sex, no involvement, nothing like that. We started hanging around and decided we liked each other. We went to her sister's house in Orlando, Fla. Stayed there for a week. Still no involvement, no sex. Then all of a sudden we decided to get married. So we got married." Mike claims getting married was "her idea." He and his wife stayed in Florida for a year while he attended college and his wife worked as a teacher. Soon their first child was born. "The child cried a lot. I would come home from school and rock her. The little girl would fall asleep, then her mother would rest. But after a while it got too much of an ordeal for me—going to college, coming home and taking care of the kid. We decided to drive out to California. Because I was retired from the Navy, we moved to San Diego where I [had easy access to] the Navy Hospital [and could use] all my Navy privileges. Then we had our second child. I got a job at the Navy Exchange, stayed there until I retired, and took care of the family. In the meantime we had another child." Mike never had sex with men while he was married. Recalling his divorce, he says, "I didn't love her anymore. I was more of a father than a husband." At the time of their separation in 1976, Mike's wife and children, ages 4, 6, and 8, returned to Florida to live. Mike no longer has contact with his ex-wife. "We used to talk about the kids. I called the kids every week while they were in Florida. When they got older—got to high school, got to work, everything like that—I switched to calling once a month. I still call them once a month."

Ben Fowler's marriage was also linked to his military career. "I was in the military in Kansas City. I'd been in a straight singles group, dating this nice woman. Then I was going to the gay bars afterward. I...was 39 years old and getting the social pressure of being 39 and not married." He got married in 1962 but did not tell his wife he was gay. Later, after he retired from the service, he remembers, "I'd go to the Air Force base to play golf, play just nine holes, get a bottle of vodka, and go to the tubs in Kansas City, and then come home at dinnertime very inebriated. 'Something is going on; we need to talk,' my wife would say, and I'd reply, 'I don't want to talk about it.' One night I was supposed to be figure skating. She checked all three figure-skating rinks. I was not at any of them." As a result of that confrontation, Ben told his wife that he was gay. She was "stunned," and they went to a marriage counselor, who asked, "'What do you want to be? You've got 20 years left in your life.'" The choices were clear to Ben: "I could stay married and pretend, or dissolve the marriage. I decided it was time to finally be honest about who I was." Ben and his wife separated in 1980 and divorced two years later. They remain friends.

LESBIANS

"Lesbians—they love me!"

—*José Sarría*

The relationship between gay men and lesbians has at times been uneasy. On the one hand, gay men and lesbians face similar issues and often want to present themselves as a united front. On the other hand, gay men and lesbians often find it difficult to see eye to eye. Not surprisingly, the 41 men expressed an array of feelings about lesbians.

George Casper likes the lesbians he socializes with. "I think the relationships are very good." Robert of Palm Desert says, "I've enjoyed their company." And Mike states unequivocally, "I don't mind them a bit. They're women. A woman's a woman."

Some of the men are not as accepting. Lesbians "can be very overpowering," observes Ben Fowler. "I've seen organizations where they often take control, but that's a whole other story." John Peters concurs: "Some of them [lesbians] overdo it in my book, carrying on in public, like in church. I often go to the MCC [Metropolitan Community Church] in Davenport [Iowa], and I don't appreciate when they've got to sit there hugging and hugging during church. I think that's awful." Norman Eckelberger says, "I do not like a woman who thinks she's a football player, the type that's gonna beat the heck out of you. But if a woman acts feminine, like a woman is supposed to act—in my way of thinking, how she's supposed to act—I accept her very well." Ed Conlon opines, "I do not appreciate the overmasculinity that is shown, the swearing. Not that I am prudish, but the crudeness I just don't appreciate. However, I don't condemn it because it is their life. I do not judge." Frank Poe says that he has known only four lesbians and "can't stand" two of them.

Some of the men have mixed or evolving feelings regarding lesbians. Jim Mitchell admits, "There was a time when it was hard to reach out to lesbians. I spent summers in the '60s and '70s at Cherry Grove on Fire Island. In those days the lesbians who were there kept to themselves. But more recently…it's become a much more integrated group." Jim is upbeat about his current relations with lesbians. "I like the lesbians I meet," he says. "We get along very well." Lee Denman is gradually becoming more comfortable with lesbians. "It's only recently I've met some that I consider people." He adds, though, "We have several very nice lesbian couples that we are friends with who come into the bar." Will Belais is put off by what he sees as some lesbians' personal habits. "I find lesbians interesting, but I don't know any really close. Most gay men—I know, this is a stereotype—take care of their bodies; they like to be well-dressed. But lesbians will do anything to make themselves as ugly as they can be. I get tired of it; I can't stand it."

Clee says he likes to talk to women. Fred, though, feels that lesbians can be "difficult" and there are "only about three sets that we're really friendly with." But Clee adds, "We always invite lesbians to a party to make the mix look close to a straight mix."

FAMILY OF ORIGIN

"My father was very resentful of me being gay. Ours wasn't a terribly close relationship."

—*Jon Borset*

For every gay man, regardless of his age, issues can arise concerning his family of origin. Even in today's society, which is more accepting of homosexuality, coming out places a strain on family relationships. Many of the men interviewed are lucky; their families have been supportive. But this is certainly not the case for all of the men.

José Sarría is one of the men with a supportive family. "They know who I am. They're very proud of me. They see me on television. I'm told of anything that happens in the family. I'm not rejected."

Ed of Oakland also has an accepting family. "They took Bob [Ed's partner] in as a member of the family, and Bob's family took me in. We never had a sign on our backs. You hear the current lingo from people who are much younger: 'I came out to my family.' I never sat down with my parents and said, 'I am gay.' I brought Bob into my life 55 years ago. My parents knew I lived with another man and they accepted him. My brother, a physician, was a little uneasy at one time and asked my mother [if she thought] I should get married. But that was about it."

Unlike Ed, Norm Self did officially come out to his family. "Coming out to my sisters was a bit of a jolt, but they took it graciously. I think the net effect has been positive. They and my ex-wife took it graciously and reaffirmed their love for me." Norm continues, "I get along wonderfully with my family. We have very different lifestyles and philosophical views on things, but we love each other and get along fine when we're together. We're just not motivated to be together a lot." Norm admits that coming out had not exactly been a revelation to any of his family members. "Each of them said, 'Well, it's not a total surprise.' But suspicion and reality are two different things, so [coming out brought on] a new level of testing and trust."

Ed Conlon feels that he "relates very well" to the remaining members of his family of origin. "I am openly gay to members of my family, and they accept it." He cites a visit from a 56-year-old female cousin he had not seen in more than 40 years, "She came in knowing I was gay, though we never discussed it." Alluding to his partner, he adds, "Over the years I always signed the Christmas cards 'Eddie and Shawne.'"

When Ben Fowler divorced his wife in 1982, he sent out Christmas cards with a note that said, "I'm finally being honest about who I am." Most of the reactions he got were favorable. "All of my relatives and most of my friends said, 'We're happy for you.'

I lost a few friends, but most said, 'Come and visit.'" Although Ben has a lesbian sister, he hasn't talked to her in several years. He characterizes her as "a very angry person—angry at me, angry at our parents, angry at doctors and lawyers. I don't have time for angry people." Still, he considers their estrangement unfortunate. "I feel badly that we're not friendly."

Bud Jordan says his family of origin knows he is gay. "They found out many years ago. I didn't tell them—didn't feel it was my place to tell them. But they found out, and they all rallied around me. I've never had a problem." Bud notes that his family welcomed his partner, Vic, as well as the couple's circle of friends.

Many of the men have avoided familial conflict by not disclosing their sexuality. Frank Poe is a good example. He says of his family, "They're all dead, but when they were alive, I got along with them just fine. I kept my secret about being gay." John Peters puts it this way: "Most of my family don't know that I fool around."

Norman Eckelberger has seen a gradual improvement in his relationship with his family of origin. "When I was in my early 20s, my family didn't quite accept me." Now, however, he believes they accept him fairly well. Jim also views his family relations as "pretty good" as long as some degree of distance is maintained. "We call on the phone. I stay here; they stay there." George Casper says his family relations are favorable with one exception: "My son's wife does not like or approve of gay people and she does not like or approve of me." But George's son is OK with his father being gay.

Bill Strong characterizes his family relations as "split," noting, "I get along very well with some of them, and with some I do not." He adds, "For approximately 10 years I didn't speak a word to three of them." Included among those three were his children.

Cyprian Fary and Steve Scott both have trouble relating to their families of origin. "I've been away from them for so many years," Cyprian explains. "I left when I was very young and never got back until after 31 years. During the 31 years everything changed—the town, the people. The people I went to school with—I can't even find them." Steve Scott sees two primary reasons for his rift with his family: "Number one, the distance. And number two, the Mormon church…. I'm not close to my family at all."

STRAIGHT PEOPLE

"I don't like being around straight men very much, especially in social settings. I find it very awkward and uncomfortable. I avoid all social gatherings of men who are straight. We have a men's group in my church, and I won't go to it."

—Will Belais

The 41 men express varying degrees of comfort in dealing with straight people. Some, like Will Belais, are uncomfortable around straight men. Many of the interviewees say they enjoy the company of women more than men. Others, like Jim Mitchell, claim they get along with everyone. "I have no problem. I was president of my union: a large union of 1,100 people, the vast majority of them straight."

Like John Mitchell, John Schiappi has had chiefly positive dealings with straight people. "I thought that if people knew that I was gay or alcoholic, I would be rejected," he says. "Just the opposite has been true. Every year, the shareholders of my employee-owned company elect 12 employees for the board of directors. The year after I came out as a gay man and came to terms with being alcoholic, I was reelected to the board with more votes than I had received the year before…. Now that everybody knows I'm gay, it's much easier to have a good friendship with women because the sexual issue is taken out."

Norm Self also feels comfortable with both gays and straights. "All my life I've been straight to all appearances, and I'm a gregarious person, so I have lots of good connections with straight people." Based on his experience in two straight marriages and observations of gay couples, Norm sees "some very significant differences between gay and straight couples, but I get along fine in either context." Regarding women's issues he adds, "I've been a feminist all my conscious life."

Much of Fred and Clee's social life has been spent in mixed company. Clee says, "I relate very well. I mix; I don't wear a sign when I go to a party. If they find out, that's their problem." Fred notes, "Having been married twice, I'm able to slide through. As far as the neighborhood is concerned, over many years you get to know the people. Maybe there'd be a Christmas party or something like that. We've never had trouble with our neighbors regarding our relationship or anything."

A few interviewees spend more time socializing with straights than gays. Richard Malloy "never uses the word 'straight.'" He describes most of his friends as "nongay." Mel Clark and his partner also associate with straights more than gays and have hosted parties and fund-raisers and regularly invite a mix of gay and straight guests. Mel relates why one man once declined an invitation: "One fellow said later, 'I didn't come to your party because I don't go to mixed parties. How can you have a party where there

are gay people and straight people?' He couldn't understand that."
Mel recollects a fund-raiser he and his partner hosted for a local
hospice: "We invited our neighbors, put an ad in the newspaper.
The woman president of the hospice would not attend 'because
you're having straight people there.' We ended up holding the hospice fund-raising dinner over two nights. Friday night was for
everyone: straight, gay, the whole bit. We had a wonderful crowd—
wonderful time. Saturday night was all gay, and it was kind of blah.
It wasn't nearly as much fun as having straight people, when our
neighbors brought their kids."

Many of the men commented on their comfort level with
women. Tom Pait says he has "lots of women friends." Ed Conlon
"adores women" and points to the objets d'art in his apartment as
proof of his admiration. "If you look about my living room, and as
you go through my house, you will see a collection of women's
portraits, porcelain figures of women, Austrian statues of women.
You will see framed portraits of women. I think women are wonderful." Lee Denman says, "Women in general—especially ones in
business—I relate to very well. In fact, I've done consulting for
women, and I've worked for them." Norman Eckelberger says he
relates well to both straights and gays, but he actively seeks
women friends. "I definitely want their companionship, because I'd
dislike living in a world of all men. I need some female companionship."

Jim Edmonds has a woman friend he has been "going out
with since 1962" and doing things like attending symphony
concerts together. "We still go out to dinner every Friday if I'm
at home. She was the one who took me to the hospital when I
had heart surgery, stayed there with me, and called my family
back in Massachusetts. Her family—her husband was in my

drama department—has been like my second family. We were a two-piano team for 25 years, traveled together, and had some interesting experiences." Jim thinks his affection for women comes from his longtime membership in a professional organization, the state music teachers association. "Almost all of the members are women," he says.

CHAPTER 7

Relationships

LONG-TERM RELATIONSHIPS

"Vic and I lived together for 42 years—shared everything, owned everything together, had one bank account."

—Bud Jordan

L ess than half of the 41 men interviewed are currently in a relationship, but nearly all of them have at least some history of being in relationships with other men. Ongoing relationships range from those of a few years' duration to men who have been together more than 50 years. The men in long-term relationships are split on the issue of gay marriage: Most feel it's not necessary. But they generally are in favor of domestic-partner benefits and other legal protections for gay couples. Most of the men describe the financial and domestic portion of their relationships in terms that legally married straight couples might also use.

In 1994, Bud Jordan lost his partner, Vic, who was 11 years his senior. They met over breakfast in 1953 and were inseparable for 42 years. "We put all our money together. If he made more than

I did, fine; if I made more than he did, fine; but it all went in one pot. If I had $500 one day, we'd put it in the bank, if he had an extra $500 the next day, we'd put it in the same bank account." Bud recalls the events leading up to Vic's unexpected death: "He'd had gout for a couple of weeks. I took care of him. It was one hell of a thing; he couldn't walk or do anything. I took him to the hospital, and he came home after an overnight stay. The next day, he got up and said, 'Bud, I think I'm going to have to go to the hospital again—I'm feeling really bad. So we go to Emergency. They were working on him, and I left because I thought you don't die of gout, so I left saying, 'I'll see you in a little while, babe.' That's the last time I saw him." When Bud asked about the cause of death, a nurse told him too much acid had been taken out of Vic's system." A little regretfully, Bud adds, "I did not sue for malpractice. I've had people ask me why not. I said, 'No, I don't want to go through it.' I just didn't. I should've, I guess."

The reality of the situation, of course, was that because Bud was not Vic's spouse in the eyes of the law, he probably had no legal grounds to sue. It also meant that he couldn't collect the Social Security survivor benefits that widowed spouses routinely receive. Bud says, "When Vic passed away, our income together was about $3,000 a month. I lost $1,700 in monthly Social Security checks by him passing away. Even my family—they're very religious, but they accepted us—all thought the same thing, that I should get his Social Security. 'That is not right,' they said. 'You two earned that money together and you should have it.'" Bud is now a strong supporter of gay marriage and extending domestic-partner benefits to same-sex couples.

Charles had a 42-year relationship that ended with his partner's death in 1998. "We were very happy. We got along, although some people considered us both to be cold fish." Charles says he and his partner tried not to be overly possessive of each other. "Since we both worked, all of our time together was not devoted to each other. We were very adamant about [each of us] having our own group of friends." Charles says they lived together in his house, and that money was "split right down the middle—we never haggled about money." Charles's views on legal recognition of gay couples are diametrically opposed to Bud's. Charles dislikes the term "gay marriage" for committed gay couples and considers the extension of domestic-partner benefits to gay and lesbian couples a "distortion."

Ed of Oakland met Bob, his partner of 55 years, after World War II, when they both worked for the Veterans Administration in Los Angeles. Ed recalls: "I went back to Columbia University in 1946, finished, and wanted to get the hell out of New York. I came west with a New York City friend of mine, whom I lived with for six months. Then I met Bob, and we've been together ever since." At first, Ed and Bob kept separate apartments in Los Angeles. They then bought a house where they lived for nearly 10 years before moving to San Francisco. "We saw the smog coming in. We were tired of Los Angeles getting bigger and smoggier. In 1958, we had the opportunity to move north, to San Francisco, and we loved it." When asked about gay marriage, Ed says, "I don't think I need that." He goes on to clarify his stance: "We grew up in a community that rejected us as an identified body. Gradually, slowly, that's changing. Twenty-five years from now it may be quite normal for gay people to have a church marriage and benefits built into the contract." He admits, "I'm a poor one to envisage how I might feel about [gay marriage] because I'm the result of 83 years of many negative experiences— people making fun of faggots."

Richard Malloy and his partner, Tucker, who are a year apart in age, consider their 54-year relationship a marriage. However, they would not want to make their marriage legal. "We're against legalized [gay] marriage—too much pork in it, and it hasn't worked with nongay people, so we have to find our own niche and our own way of doing it. Everybody's free to do what they want to do. We just do not want marriage. For 54 years we've survived fine." Richard explains how they've improvised some of the legal protections afforded to heterosexual married couples. "We did a legal adoption of Tucker because I have a sister who would jump in at any point—cheat me out of a lot of money. I call her my ex-sister." As an added protection Richard and Tucker own everything jointly. "Even the car—everything is joint."

Ed Conlon describes his relationship history: "In the beginning, I was very promiscuous and fell in love in the Navy, when I was 17. Always wanting to recapture that love—I never realized you can't do that; you can't substitute somebody else for the first love in your life. There was a five-year period when I drank in straight bars and, oddly, had a three-year affair or commitment with a straight person, my second love. I was constantly disappointed in relationships, up until the time that I met my present life partner, Shawne. Then, at 34 years old, I decided to settle down and really work at it. I did, and it has been the most wonderful thing."

Ed and Shawne have now been together for 41 years. Ed says that early in their relationship his mother would "introduce the two of us as 'Eddie and his friend,' then she went to 'Eddie and my adopted son,' and finally she simply introduced the two of us as 'my sons.' When my mother was dying, she asked me to promise her that 'you and Shawne will always be together and watch out for each other.' I said, 'After 17 years, do you think we would not stay together and take care of one another?'" Ed adds, "I never realized that you can love someone more than you do until I became ill. Then I saw how tender Shawne was and how caring. I saw the hurt and the worry in his face, and it drew me closer to him. I looked at him one day and said, 'I never thought I could love you more than I do, or did, but I do.' Being ill with cancer gave me more love than I knew I had for him."

Ed and Shawne own everything together. "I own nothing; he owns nothing. We share everything. Money, objects—it's a sharing." Ed would legally marry Shawne if it were possible and thinks that domestic-partner benefits are "wonderful, an advancement that we need." When asked about California's domestic-partner registration law, Ed says, "You take what you get, run with it, and be grateful for it. We did not have the domestic-partner law before and do now. Shawne and I carry our California Certificate of Domestic Partnership in our wallets. As soon as it was available, we applied; our certificate is number 299. That means we were the 299th couple in California who were issued a certificate."

Frank Poe cherishes his memories of his relationship of over 20 years with Ed Wright. "The most important relationship I had was with Ed, who died about four years ago. I was very devoted to him. Before that, I didn't have any relationships." Ed was eight years younger than Frank. They met in a Southern California gay bar. Frank remembers: "I was living in an apartment in [Los Angeles's] Wilshire district. After we got to know each other, he [Ed] wanted me to move to a house in Monterey Park, but he said, 'This house isn't a good house. I'm going to get rid of it and get another one.' He did, and I moved in with him." Later on, they moved to Palm Springs. They "slept in the same bed" and spent most of their time together. Frank recalls that Ed "always took care of the bills, but when he got older and just a little senile, I took over."

Fred and Clee have been together for 48 years. Clee describes their relationship as "very close, very, very loving." Their "early life was quite sexual," he recalls, but that "diminishes as time goes on." They met in a Los Angeles restaurant where Clee was creating a stained-glass window. "Fred would come in for breakfast before I started work. I think one of the important things in a relationship is to let your partner show his own talents rather than dominating the person. Let him make himself and you make yourself." Fred and Clee have always jointly managed their money. Fred remembers when they opened their first joint bank account: "We kept a count on it, but after a few years you realize that you've established what each one wants to be responsible for. Like, I pay the real estate taxes and the house insurance, and Clee pays for the car insurance, groceries, and garbage pickup." Although they both consider gay marriage a "false premise," Fred and Clee see the extension of domestic-partner benefits to gay couples as "long overdue."

It was at work that Warde Laidman met his partner, Hadley Dale Hall, who is three years his junior. "It's been a relationship of approximately 38 years," Warde says, "and by and large it's been a monogamous relationship." Warde considers the relationship his "first," noting that he had "some relationships when I was in my teens, but I really didn't understand the context." Warde and Hadley have combined their financial resources. They both retired in 1987, and now they "plan ahead together for vacations and time away. We go over our calendars—we keep joint calendars so that one knows what the other is doing—together at the start of the week." At this point in his relationship, Warde says gay marriage is "not a major thing," but he's in favor domestic partnerships, which he sees as an alternative to marriage.

Bill Strong was married to his wife for 29 years. He is now 17 years into his first relationship with a man 10 years his junior. "We get along very well. I love him very much, and I feel he loves me very much." Bill says they are mostly stay-at-homes, but they do recreational things together. and also share expenses. "We contribute to the pot; that's worked out very well. If one of us has a little more money, he just naturally puts a little more into the pot." Notwithstanding his commitment to his partner, Bill asserts that gay marriage is not for him. "I have a problem with that word, 'marriage.' 'Relationships,' 'companion,' or just about any other word would be fine with me, but I have a problem with the 'marriage' word." He feels that domestic partnerships are an alternative to marriage and wishes the extension of domestic-partner benefits "would happen a lot quicker, at a more rapid pace. But all things in due time."

Ben Fowler was married to a woman for much of his life, from ages 39 to 67, but he had not been in a gay relationship prior to meeting Lee on the Internet. Committing to a gay relationship, Ben says, "was a big decision when I decided to go for it. We corresponded. Lee was in an 18-year relationship when his partner died of a heart attack." The two of them visited "up and down the West Coast" until Lee moved in with Ben. Although they live together, they manage their money separately. "Lee inherited some money, and he's saved money and is not working now but plans to," Ben says. "In the relationship we share the duties: He cooks, and I do the dishes. We sleep in the same room, but he has his computers in his room, and I have my computer in my room." Because of the time they spend on their computers, Ben admits, "Most of the time we're in separate rooms, about a quarter of the time we're together." Ben remains leery of gay marriage. "I don't think we need to call it 'marriage' as heterosexuals do. I'd rather say 'gay unions.'" He's "all for" domestic partnerships, which he views as an alternative to more formal unions for gay men.

Robert Bettinger was also married to a woman. After his divorce and coming out, Robert was with a lover, "who has since died of AIDS. Then I had a lover who was a real estate person, who has also died of AIDS." Alone for several years, Robert went through some brief affairs, which he characterizes as "disasters," before moving to Florida, where he met his current lover, 21 years his junior. They now live on a salt-marsh wetlands nature preserve in San Diego County, Calif., and have been together for five years. Robert describes his lover as "making a career transition and navigating a midlife crisis at age 50. He's focusing on being a yoga teacher, a previous occupation he practiced, and wants to continue [doing] that. So he's doing yoga five days a week and building up a private practice." Robert adds, "When he was in school I took care of all the money except for his car. Now that he's out of school, he does half the cooking and half of the volunteer work. I provide the major income for expenses, and I do repairs around the house too. He's not handy that way. Our arrangements are in transition. Things work better now that he's out of school." Living in a "400-square-foot environment with another person" affects the relationship, Robert says. "For me, it's beautiful. For him, it's not as easy. We recently changed from a motor home of about 200 square feet to a trailer of almost 400 square feet, with a washer-dryer, dishwasher, ceiling fans, built-in vacuum cleaner, and space. We have a custom-built trailer, high ceilings, a great view. For me, it's just right." When asked about gay marriage, Robert says, "I'm in a relationship. I feel responsible, as my father was responsible with my mother. I don't really know whether I want marriage or not." Domestic-partner benefits, on the other hand, are viewed by Robert as "absolutely essential, fine—the more, the better—as only a fair and just thing."

John Kiley and his partner, Gene, have been together for 48 years. A native of Australia, John met Gene after he had been in the United States for about 18 months. "I met Gene, and we've been together ever since. We share everything, including money. We're together most of the time and generally agree about what we're going to do. We both have some specific interests. For example, if I'm swimming in a meet, Gene will come along. If he is in a running event, I'll go along. We support one another in whatever we do." John says he would be in favor of gay marriage for the tax benefits but adds, "We've never felt the need for any certificate to say that we're married. We have our relationship, and it's solid."

UNATTACHED

"I'd get married in a heartbeat. I really would like to use the word *marriage*. I would like to look at people and say, 'We are married. This is a wedding.'"

—*Will Belais*

The men not currently in a long-term relationship are split on the issue of whether they want one. Like the men in relationships, their opinions on gay marriage and domestic partnerships vary. Most favor the institution of domestic partnerships and other legal protections, if not actual marriage.

Will Belais is not currently in a relationship. "I wish I were, though. I had a friend for a decade. We saw each other almost every day but didn't live together. He told me he was cruising one day in the men's room and he'd met somebody. I knew that person, that he was HIV-positive. I had to stop seeing my friend—I simply couldn't deal with it." Now, Will shares his home with a housemate in a nonsexual arrangement that is "more like a father-son relationship." Will is still actively seeking a relationship, because he likes the idea of living in a family setting with another man, somebody he "can enjoy, argue with, do all the things that families do—a man I can introduce with great pride." Will is active in several groups that help him meet men, and he runs an ad on the Internet. "I've done pretty well on the Internet," he says. "I've had 50 to 60 responses." Will feels he can remain fairly selective. "I decided if they couldn't spell in English, I wouldn't write to them, or if they sounded hokey or stupid, or if they talked dirty to me, I wouldn't answer. It's been a very effective ad. I was straightforward—I mean, I didn't talk about how beautiful I was. I talked about the things I cherish, and if you want to cherish them with me, I'd be glad to [meet you]." Will says he is interested in one of his neighbors, but the man "owns a house in West Virginia and goes there every weekend—a commitment I can't make." Another local man he likes is married, and Will finds that limiting. Will likes the idea of gay marriage and feels that domestic-partner benefits are an "about-time issue." He cites the case of a longtime friend whose partner died without a will. "The things they had built together and purchased together were just ripped away from him by his late partner's parents without recourse."

John Schiappi is not nearly as interested as Will in having a traditional long-term relationship. He says he has had only one live-in lover, a man 20 years his junior whom he met at work. The relationship lasted about a year. "He was very sexually promiscuous, sometimes staying out until 2 or 3 in the morning, sometimes not coming home at all." John felt his partner's behavior "was becoming a threat to my sobriety, so I ended the relationship." About six months later, though, they got back together, albeit on different terms. "We resumed a relationship in which we dated on weekends, and he would sometimes spend the night. That was much easier to handle because I didn't have to concern myself with what he might be doing at other times." John has also just ended "a three-year relationship with a man in Holland, kind of ideal in the sense of logistics. One year, for instance, we were together on five different occasions for a week or two each time—him coming here, our traveling together, or me going to Holland. That type of relationship I can handle." John says he is not interested in a permanent live-in relationship, "whether it's marriage or otherwise," but admits that "if the perfect man came along, I might change my mind."

Jim of Michigan spent 12½ years in a relationship that he had believed was monogamous. "But then I found out he was cheating on me." Jim ended the relationship several years ago. His other relationships have been of much shorter duration. "I'm not really for gay marriage," he says. Jim views domestic-partner benefits as "really good for some people," though.

George of New York City, who is not currently in a relationship, says his views on gay marriage have changed over time. "I was a gay activist in the '70s and '80s, and I didn't think it was an important issue for us. Today, I think marriage is an important issue. I would opt for marriage." He sees domestic-partner benefits as "only a matter of justice, like the *Brown* v. *Board of Education*

U.S. Supreme Court case on schooling. It's the 'separate but equal' treatment that ends up not equal."

RELATIONSHIP VARIATIONS

"It's a different kind of relationship, I'm with Steve four days a week at his house, and [away from him] three days at my own house."

—*Norman Eckelberger*

Because gay relationships have historically not been accepted by society, there hasn't been the need for them to conform to an established norm. There is no set way for men to begin a relationship or to be together. Norman Eckelberger and Steve Scott provide an excellent example. The pair live together part of the week and apart during the rest of the week. Steve says, "A lot of people ask if we are in a relationship. I guess you would have to call it that—a strange type of relationship. I don't mean we run around sexually. But…I'm not ready for a seven-days-a-week relationship."

Norm Self sees himself "at the lead edge of what I think may become a relationship. As it happens, he's younger almost by 20 years. He's a professional person in social services, a very spiritual person." They met at a personal enrichment workshop and made "a good connection there." Afterward, they didn't see each other for two years, "then suddenly got back in the same geography and just clicked. Like any relationship that's going to happen, it begins with chemistry, and we've got a little flicker of chemistry going. When we looked beyond that, we discovered some real common bonds that show a lot of promise."

Bill Worrall also feels that he could be on the verge of a love relationship. He describes his friendship with the man he is interested in as "tentative right now. It's not what I call a relationship yet. It may happen."

Tom Pait says he is in a "semi-relationship" with a man in his 50s. "We get together every few weeks, watch a movie, and get it on. We enjoy each other a lot. We enjoy sex together." Both men are athletic and enjoy outdoor activities. "He swims in the bay every day, and I go down there and watch him. Sometimes I'll join him in the bay." Tom says they also like to "just talk about everyday things." Usually, they combine resources to pay for recreation, but sometimes they go dutch.

"Yes and no" is Mike's reply when asked whether he is currently in a relationship with a man. "I go with this gentleman, a friend of 55 that I met at the beach. We've known each other for 10 years, but we just started [having] sex maybe a year and a half ago. Every so often—he's a painter and has a truck—he'll take me for a ride. He grabs my leg and grabs my cock, and we have sex—maybe every two weeks. He's in love with me. He's never had homosexual sex before but loves it now." Mike says they go to "his place and mine," usually after chance meetings. His friend wants regular meetings; Mike doesn't, though, because his friend "wants sex every night, and I don't want it every night. I just can't do it." Seeing each other in a nonsexual context isn't really an option, Mike says, because "when we go out to a movie or do anything else, the first thing he does is grab my cock. He always wants sex." Mike firmly believes in extending domestic-partner benefits to gay and lesbian couples. "It should be the same for everybody," he states. "I don't think there should be any difference."

Intergenerational Relationships

> "In my 60s I discovered young men coming out of the woodwork who thought I was the best thing since vanilla ice cream!"
>
> —*George Casper*

The phenomenon of younger men being attracted to older men is in full bloom for many of the 41 men interviewed. While a few men have not had the experience of younger men being attracted to them, most have—to varying degrees and with varying degrees of mutuality.

George Casper enjoys the attention he receives from younger men. "By the time I reached 50, I wasn't successful any longer in finding partners—not one-night stands but 'partners.' I thought my sex life was coming to an end. My 50s were kind of a wasteland." George says this changed dramatically in his 60s. "It's been marvelous, wonderful, good for my self-esteem. I love it!"

John Peters says of younger men being attracted to him, "I have no problem with it. I love it." Bill Worrall enthuses, "As I get older—and my hair's silver now—I'm getting more attention from the 20- to 40-year-olds than I've ever got." Ben Fowler reports that young men regularly visit his full-leather Web site; "I just eat it up," he gloats. Mike says young men are attracted to him, but he wonders why. "I have no idea why they're attracted to me, but they are." Robert Bettinger supposes that "it's very common" for younger men to be attracted to him and adds, "It would be easy for me to have sex with a lot of younger men."

Not all of the men, however, are quite so enthusiastic about attention from younger men. "Younger people go for me," notes Tom Pait. "They always want something, or you don't trust them. So I just wait and find somebody that's a little older." Robert of Palm Desert has already met a few younger men who were interested in him but has chosen to keep his distance. "I have no problems, and I don't want their problems." Jim Edmonds says he's not interested in "anyone under 40. I want somebody that can be an equal and share experiences." Steve Scott even sounds a little peeved by the easy availability of 20-somethings: "If they are really young: 20, 25—and there's a lot of them here, younger guys who like older guys—I'm not attracted." Norman Eckelberger doesn't "care for the young mind" and quips, "I don't want to raise them." Likewise, Fred has dismissed advances from younger men. "I just don't want to deal with it," he says.

During his years of working abroad, Lee Denman found it common for younger men to consider him attractive. "There was never a problem having a playmate overseas," he confides. He has found it more difficult to meet younger men since his return to the United States. To be sure, there are plenty of younger men in and around Lee's adopted home of Oceanside, Calif.—the U.S. Marine Corps Base at Camp Pendleton is only a few miles away. But the Capri Lounge's high-profile location in downtown Oceanside drives away gay or bisexual enlisted men. Lee explains, "Since the bar is right in the middle of town, the Marines are very hesitant to be seen going in or out. Most of the gay Marines go down to San Diego."

José Sarría thinks younger men who are attracted to older men may be looking for a father figure. "They just like you, or lack affection from their father, or didn't have a father. Some of them are attracted to me not as a man but as a mother or grandma. 'You remind me of my grandmother,' they say, and I take that as a compliment."

Similarly, Ed Conlon finds that that many younger men are attracted to him because of his public persona as Queen Eddie. And because he usually makes it plain that he's already in a relationship, they feel comfortable being casually affectionate with him. "They know that I have a lover and I am not a threat to them, which they might feel about some older men." Not being a threat, he says, means he "will get patted on the rump and such." Still, Ed has encountered "two younger men that had a serious attraction toward me sexually." One desired Ed the man; the other, Queen Eddie.

GAY VS. STRAIGHT RELATIONSHIPS

"I don't see why we should conform to the same set of rules that people expect of straight relationships."

—*Jim Edmonds*

There is no question that gay relationships differ from their straight counterparts. The lack of legal protection for gay couples is one major distinction. Others include decision-making power and allocation of domestic and financial responsibility. All of which brings up the oft-repeated question: Can two men make it work? Opinions among the men interviewed vary. Only one man,

Charles, felt overwhelmingly pessimistic about the success of gay male relationships. "I don't think gay relationships work. What I've read and keep hearing is that some [gay] people consider anything over five years long-term, and that's too transient for my temperament."

The rest of the 41 men are more optimistic. Mike, who was formerly married to a woman, views gay relationships as "marvelous, much better" than relationships with the opposite sex. "That's true because I think a man knows what another man wants. A man will tell another man what he wants, what to do, what not to do, what he does want, what he doesn't want." He confides that his relationship with his wife, especially in regard to sex, was not like that.

George Casper considers most comparisons between gay and straight relationships irrelevant. "I think [a gay relationships is] a very different phenomenon in many ways. Two men don't go about things the same way that a man and a woman do. There's not the same kind of interaction emotionally and intellectually."

Jim Mitchell takes into account broader social trends. "If we go by what sociologists say and what the statistics show, about one half of straight relationships end in divorce." Consequently, Jim concludes, "I don't see anything inherently better in a straight relationship than a gay one." Tom Pait agrees: "I think there are more unhappy straight relationships than there are unhappy gay relationships." Likewise, John Peters says, "Most gay relationships are better than straight relationships. There's no divorce involved. It seems to me that gay men get along a lot better in a relationship than straights do." Gay relationships would work "just fine if society would leave us alone," says Frank Poe. "But there are too many ultra-Christian conservatives that don't like us."

Some of the men feel that gay relationships work partly because gay men have a more relaxed approach toward sex outside of a committed relationship, and that this helps gay relationships work. "I think strain in straight marriages would occur much less frequently if women were as receptive to extracurricular sex as men are," says John Schiappi. Will Belais agrees: "We use words like 'promiscuity,' but I think men need multiple partners—that we learn from multiple partners." Bill Worrall says, "I've heard the statistic that 50% of straight marriages end up in divorce, and I feel I may know the answer: Some girls are 'saving it until marriage,' [so] some people get married without having sex first. Sex is such an important part of marriage that if the sex doesn't work, the rest of it's not going to work, either."

Lee Denman, on the other hand, believes gay men in relationships need to learn the difference between "lust and love." Despite this reservation he says, "I think gay relationships work just as well as straight ones. I've met many gay couples who've been together for a good many years."

Ed Conlon has advised numerous men and women about gay relationships through his column, "Ask Queen Eddie," which regularly appears in a San Diego gay and lesbian newspaper. He sees very little difference between gay relationships and straight relationships. "Love is basic; the problems we have are basic. One thing gays don't have on the whole is the responsibility of raising children [or saving] college funds for children." Everything else, he feels, is relevant to both gay and straight relationships.

Bill Strong voices a similar opinion. Any relationship can succeed "if you work at it and both parties are very interested in keeping the relationship going." Milton Lestz concurs. "It depends on the people. Some straight relationships don't work; [the man

and woman] just stay together for the children or whatever—
the same [goes] for gays. I don't think there's a huge difference."
Jim of Michigan, who believes that in general "lesbian relationships work better than gay [male] relationships," also points out
that to succeed "it just takes a real commitment."

CHAPTER 8

Sex

THE IMPORTANCE OF SEX

"If I had a partner, I would get more of it."

—Bill Worrall

Sex is important to gay men of all ages. After all, a preference for romantic and sexual contact with other men is what sets gays apart as a group. The 41 men interviewed for this book are no exception. Most report they are satisfied with the amount and quality of sex they have, although many concede their sex drive has decreased with age. Recently, Viagra has made a strong impact on the sex lives of some of the men.

Ron Dropkin is satisfied with his sex life. "At different times in my life, like when I was single, I have been involved in most sexual acts that gay men are involved in." He adds, "My sex drive at this point in life is not the same as it was earlier." Ron's sex life is now centered on his partner of 15 years. "We're very devoted to one another and have a real bonding. The relationship has grown beyond sex."

Fred and Clee agree that sex is important in their relationship. Clee calls it "showing love." Fred no longer considers passionate sex as important as it used to be, but he's come to cherish "contact, touching your partner on the shoulder or grabbing his hand when you go by, or patting him on the head." Lee Denman expresses a similar sentiment. "Sex is always fun, but it doesn't make the world go around." For Ben Fowler, sex is not as important "as it is to a lot of people." He says his "sex drive has decreased to some degree" and therefore has become "fearful of just not being able to perform."

Conversely, John Schiappi says, "I'm 71 and I'm still doing compulsive cruising, an issue I've struggled and wrestled with all my life. But lately I'm thinking that the compulsive sex adds a zest to my life, something that I would not want missing. My current friendship with a Dutch man began with my thinking in compulsive sexual terms, and now we're into a wonderful friendship."

Some of the men feel their sex drive remains strong but isn't always fully satisfied. Jim Mitchell says, "I think about sex more than I have it. I use porno films for stimulation." Unlike some, Jim doesn't frown upon having sex buddies. "I know people, have friends, so I do that too."

When it comes to sex, Bud Jordan sounds a bit more frustrated than Jim. "Yes, sex has always been important to me, but I don't have sex much anymore. I get tricks once in a while." After his partner died, he and a friend moved to a new city together. The friend's partner died the same year as Bud's partner. All four men had known one another for 30 years. "With both of us losing our partners at the same time, we thought maybe we can make it together. We tried, but after a few months it didn't work."

Medical conditions can and do affect sexual habits. Steve Scott, for instance, experiences side-effects from medication he is taking that interfere with his sex life. "Not necessarily stimulation, erections, and stuff like that," he says, "but ejaculation—the total sex experience." Richard Malloy reports that his partner Tucker is impotent because of radiation treatments for cancer but rates their sex life still as "fair." He states, "These are things you cope with in a marriage. You take things [as they] come along and happen."

TURN-ONS

"One of the things that gives me a very rich sex life is that I have a very wide repertoire of choices and preferences."

—*Norm Self*

The kinds of sexual partners whom the 41 men interviewed find attractive vary in race, ethnicity, appearance, age, and social and cultural background, among other factors. Most of the men are clear about what turns them on and what they want.

"Ever since I came out, I've always liked older men," Jim Mitchell confesses. "When I was in my 20s, I preferred people in their 40s or 50s. Even now, I still prefer people who are at least my age or older." Jim recalls how age had been his sexual stumbling block when he was in his 20s: "It was sometimes difficult to talk an older person into going to bed with me because of the age gap." Most of Jim's sex partners and lovers have been masculine men who are smaller in stature than he is. But his last partner, he notes, was "6 foot 6 and built like a football player—but most of my partners aren't built that way." Race isn't an issue for Jim either. "My last lover was black. I've been with men of my own race and with Hispanic and Asian men, as well." Jim met one man through an ad in the newspaper. "He read my ad, called me up, and we met and got along quite well. Later I discovered that he was 36, not 51, as he'd said he was." Jim's one other exception to his preference for older men has been a student he counseled. Jim recalls the explosive situation that had brought the student to his office: "[The boy's] father had caught him in bed with another man, and beaten him. The kid, 17, was lost, didn't know where to go. Because I was an out gay person at school, he came to me for counseling. I saw him as a counselee until he was 21 and through college. All of a sudden he declared he wanted to live with me and be my partner. Because I'd been giving him so much help, I felt if I rejected him it would be devastating, so I agreed and we developed a relationship."

George Casper appreciates men with "handsome faces and trim waists" between the ages of 25 and 45. He adds, "Cultural background isn't an issue if we're only talking about short-term sex. If we're talking long-term [relationships], I like people who are intellectually stimulating to me and likely closer to my own cultural and social background."

Ben Fowler wants a "man with hair on his chest, not a twinkie, [but] younger than myself—30 to 45—Anglo-Saxon, able to speak proper English." Ben confides that his sexual outlets are with his partner, Lee, and his "Internet contacts: cybersex." Lee explains the sort of thing Ben means: "Cybersex is done at a Web site where you see and hear through a program with a camera and a microphone built-in. It's interactive, with a window for viewing the person you're speaking to."

It took Jim Edmonds a long time to recognize why he was attracted "to a certain type: round-faced, balding on top, bearded, with eyeglasses and about 40." Ninety-nine percent of the men Jim finds attractive are white. "But I think that's mainly due to the environment," he observes. "I've never been in a community large enough to have a black cultural environment."

Lee Denman freely admits that sexually he prefers "to stay with the white race" and is also "somewhat hung up on blonds." But he's also developed a hankering for Latinos. "I've met a few [Mexicans] that I might have been interested in." Lee likes his sexual partners to be aged 30 to 42, but he acknowledges that his age preference "slowly creeps up as my age creeps up."

Will Belais tidily sums up what he looks for in a partner. "I like to be around athletic young men who are active and intellectually growing. I pay attention to the face. If the eyes have a gentleness, I love it. I do not like aggressive men, men who come on so strong that I feel like I'm in a vise. I prefer that he doesn't have a gut. I shouldn't say much about that because I'm developing one and can't get rid of it. But I prefer a man who has a vigor about himself." Regarding ethnicity Will says, "I prefer Europeans, but that doesn't mean that I wouldn't have a relationship with either an African-American or an Asian. I've never had an opportunity to have that relationship, so I don't know because all my relationships have been with European-type men—Americans and those of French or German background."

"I don't look for younger men. I've always looked for men my age or older," says Jim of Michigan. "It doesn't matter so much [about] race. [He needs to be] clean and neat, somebody that's not called a slut." Jim admits to feeling a bit out of place in some gay clubs. "I went to a bar in my hometown this year for the first time in 10 years, and basically it was just children, loud music, and smoke there."

For John Peters, men who are "nice and clean, friendly, and outgoing" are the most attractive. "I don't like the recluse type," he says. "I don't go for guys that are not well-kept." John adds that age is "unimportant," but extra weight "turns me off." Similarly, Milton Lestz says that while neither age nor ethnicity matter, he prefers "thin" men.

José Sarría is more interested in personality than appearance. "I'm not of those that say [their partners] have to have short hair, white hair, green hair, and no stomach. I want someone that you can hold an intelligent conversation with, someone that can be in a group and say something constructive." Like José, Bill Worrall is not hung up on appearance either. "Somebody will say, 'You know the guy with the big ears,' and I'll reply, 'No, I don't know anybody with big ears,' because I don't look for that. I look for their heart. Their personality is what I remember, not their looks." Bill does, however, admit, "I like clean-shaven people, and I don't go with smokers or heavy drinkers—and no drugs at all."

Mike also feels that personality is more important than looks. "A man's personality will get me. If I like the man the way he is, I don't care what he looks like." Mike adds, though, "Well, I don't want him to be heavy." He also prefers gay white men over 40.

Steve Scott likes his men to be in the age range "from 30 to death. And I like Latinos, but then I like everybody—short men, thin men. But my lovers, all except one, have been as tall as I am."

Ed Conlon enjoys Latino men as well. "I have always loved Latin men, because my first lover, though he wasn't Latin, was Cherokee Indian and English. [He] had dark black hair and was bronze in his face. I've always been attracted to a darker man." Ed also says he prefers men "my own age or slightly younger."

John Schiappi goes for men who are "younger, physically attractive, and intellectually stimulating." He is "wide open" to men of other ethnicities and recalls a "lovely two weeks in Cuba that included several flings. I certainly found the Cuban men attractive. And a young man in Jakarta [Indonesia] is very interested in me."

"I don't have a type," says Norm Self, who draws a comparison between sex and food. "If my food choice is roast turkey, and I only ever eat roast turkey, I'd miss Beef Wellington. I'm open to an encounter and the spontaneity of what two people want to invent together. I've had sex partners of just about every ethnicity and age group, from calendar art bodies to old and fat, to young and skinny." Norm's sex life blossomed when he was over 50. "[I] began to open myself to being homoerotic—with the exception of one little two-night stand when I was 30—and I just figured I was low man on the totem pole for good erotic encounters. But I am surprised at the number of youthful, energetic, and exciting men who are attracted to me sexually. I also encounter some old men, long married, who are deprived and hungry for erotic touch, or maybe just the sensation of touch. Some of these men can be exciting once they have received permission to let some feeling come forward."

THE SEX ACT

"If you excite me, you'll probably have me doing a lot of things. If you don't excite me, I try to get out of it very quickly without having to do too much."

Gay male sexual practices run the gamut: masturbation, nipple play, oral sex, anal sex, and beyond. Oral sex and anal sex, perhaps the two most common practices, can be "active" (insertive) or "passive" (receptive). Some men who engage in oral sex and/or anal sex are exclusively active or passive. Active partners are usually called "tops," while passive partners are usually called "bottoms." Men who enjoy both active and passive sex often refer to themselves as "versatile." It should be noted here that a wide variety of other practices are considered "sexual" as well. In this section, the 41 men interviewed talk candidly—without attribution—about what they like to do in bed, the use of condoms, and erectile dysfunction.

One man confides, "I'm usually the top, and I'm very active in bed. I like being demonstrative, and I like someone being demonstrative with me. My current man is very active in bed, very touchy-feely, and I like that very much. I've never experienced that with anybody before." He answers, "Not really," when queried about using condoms, but he acknowledges, "I should use them more than I do." He's tried Viagra with mixed results. On one occasion the drug didn't work, he thinks, because "I really wasn't interested in the person. Another time, I had an erection for hours."

Another interviewee says, "If I were in full youth and did not have [physical problems], I would prefer being a top, but that is increasingly difficult these days." About condom use he notes, "My live-in relationship partner died of AIDS. At the time we knew about AIDS but didn't know clearly the risk factors. I probably fucked him a hundred times or more without a condom. Fortunately, I'm still HIV-negative. Being a top is my preference, but giving and getting oral sex? Yes, certainly. The deprivation of physical contact in my childhood means that hugging, kissing, and holding are major parts of sex for me." Because of his physical problems, he sometimes experiences erectile dysfunction. "Thank God for Viagra. I use the injection too, but that requires more planning and isn't available when [I'm] traveling because the medication has to be kept refrigerated. Combining Viagra with the injection guarantees performance." He sees relying on Viagra or penile injections as limiting, though. "It takes away some of the spontaneity. You can't just meet somebody on the street and say, 'Let's go to my apartment,' and begin functioning. Viagra takes up to an hour to kick in and work. The injection works in five minutes, but you can't carry that around with you."

One man admits he's always been a bottom. "Almost all my life, except with my very first lover, I've been a bottom. I like getting fucked, I like sucking cock. It can be one-way; [it] doesn't have to be mutual." He adds, "I have gotten into kinky sex on occasion...sometimes liking it, sometimes getting turned off by it because many of the people in it are such phonies. Some aren't, though. It can be fun as long as you know the people and you play safe." He recalls a scary anal sex experience with a man who did not use a condom. "I didn't know it until afterward. He said he was going to use a condom. I saw him open [the packaging], but afterward I discovered he hadn't used it." Like several of the men interviewed, this man is on medication that affects his ability to get and keep an erection, and he has also tried Viagra. "I have tried Viagra twice, but it didn't seem to have any effect because the doctor gave me 25 mg. I think the proper dosage is 50 mg."

An interviewee who is single but currently looking for a partner says, "I'm a bottom in anal sex and go both ways in oral sex. And I insist on condoms in anal sex." In the event he'd met someone and become monogamous, he observes, "At that time I would relax. But up until then [I'll always use] a condom."

Another single man says, "I used to think of myself as a bottom, have always seen myself as a bottom, and really like to be a bottom. I've been going to Body Electric in Oakland for three years. The last course I took was called "Power, Surrender, and Intimacy," and I learned I'm quite capable of being a top. But I remain strongly in favor of receptive oral sex. I just love to do it, but I also like having it done to me. I also like my nipples being played with a lot. I love a gentle kiss, like in a movie." He's also gotten more heavily into anal sex and says, "I can do [it] both ways." He strongly supports using condoms: "Absolutely." However, he recalls an early-morning encounter when he didn't use a condom and kept telling himself that wasn't smart.

One interviewee who has been with his lover for many years notes how his sexual role changed when their relationship began: "Before we met I was a bottom most of the time, and he was totally a bottom. Our becoming a couple changed the whole status of who does what, and I deviated a lot. He's always been anal-receptive and oral also. Our relationship has always been that sort of relationship, with me dominant and him subordinate." This interviewee also uses Viagra and reports no trouble getting or maintaining an erection.

Another man in a long-term relationship describes the sex he and his partner have as "primarily oral and huggy—we always were. Now we're huggy more than we're oral." He reports that his erection is "pretty good," but he "would be fascinated to see what Viagra would do." Because he is in a long-term monogamous relationship, he believes condom use "isn't applicable."

"I like to cuddle," says yet another man who's in a relationship, adding that he is versatile both orally and anally. "I like to play with tits. I like to be very active in sexual encounters. If I get spanked occasionally, that's OK. I don't mind spanking, but I'm not into a lot of what you might call extraneous things, mostly because I get such satisfaction with the other things that are happening." He uses condoms whenever "there's the possibility of transmitting body fluids" and reports no erection problems.

An interviewee who once preferred to be a top in anal sex has since switched to practicing only oral sex. "Anal sex was all I'd wanted to do until AIDS came around. I've never used condoms. I just don't think it would feel as natural. AIDS is the reason I don't do anal sex." He adds that penile implants "have taken care of getting and keeping an erection. I wanted recreational sex, and couldn't always perform, so I got an implant for casual sex. But if I like and desire the person, I have no problem [with erections]."

A single man who is sexually versatile says, "I like about all of it until we get to the really extreme stuff." He always practices "safe sex with anal penetration" but notes, "I do not use condoms in oral sex." Unlike some of the interviewees, he feels no need to try Viagra. "I have Viagra on hand but have never used it. I have no trouble getting an erection with someone I'm interested in. Keeping it is the problem."

Some men value physical affection as much as sexual release. "I like to cuddle and rub my hands all over a man's body," says one interviewee. "I'm not much into oral or anal sex. The closeness of the body is more important than the actual sex act. I don't like anything that gives pain to myself or to anybody else." He proceeds to describe a sexual encounter he had at a hotel while attending a conference: "I met this man and went to his room. We were in bed for two hours and just cuddled and talked—no orgasm at all. We were both very happy and content." He always carries condoms "just in case I meet someone, but I've never had a situation in which I've had to use them because I'm not doing anything orally or anally." Because he takes heart medication, his "erections aren't what they used to be."

"I like to make love," says one man who entered into a relationship recently. "I like foreplay. I try to make someone happy. I have always found in life that if you give your utmost to make the other person happy, if you give them what they need, happiness is returned to you a thousandfold." He enjoys oral sex, both active and passive, and does not use condoms. "If I was more promiscuous, I would [engage in] safe sex, but condoms don't turn me on. If I don't have to use them, I don't use them." Physical problems have affected his ability to have an erection "a little bit." He has used Viagra but says, "I don't like it, because after taking it one time I felt like I was on fire."

Another interviewee who is single remarks, "Essentially, I like mutual masturbation." Though experienced in oral sex, he has never engaged in anal sex. "I've never had it, don't know anything about it. A man tried it on me one time, but I don't remember what happened." He's never compared top or bottom roles in sex. "I never actually thought of it, to tell the truth." He "doesn't believe in" condoms and has a "history of erection problems" that he treats with Viagra. "When Viagra works, it keeps the erection—not an erection like I had when I was 19, but a good erection. Viagra doesn't help me to [reach] orgasm, but at least I can masturbate. It feels good, and eventually I will come."

Together with his long-term partner, another one of the men sometimes engages in three-ways. "We do everything—well, I say 'everything,' but [don't mean that] necessarily. We have oral sex and anal sex." When having three-ways, he and his partner always use condoms, but they don't when they just have sex together. He has also occasionally experienced erectile dysfunction. "I was having a problem keeping it up, but I've been taking some pills that help open up your arteries to maintain an erection. I tried Viagra once, and I did like it. My partner didn't. But the third person enjoyed sex very much because of it."

"The vanilla stuff is what I like," says a single man who describes himself as versatile in both oral sex and anal sex, although insertive anal sex just doesn't feel satisfying to him. "I don't get hard enough. My erectile function is nothing like it once was, but my partners love the way I am." He adds that sex is "just much more pleasant with Viagra. If I feel uneasy, I pop a Viagra and it works wonderfully." When asked about wearing condoms, he is adamant: "Use them!"

Another man in a long-term relationship notes, "I prefer oral sex. Other than that, I'm practically a virgin." He still experiences "absolutely no erection problem." Because he and his partner are both HIV-negative and do not have sex outside their relationship, he reasons, "We've never thought of or relied on the use of condoms."

"I masturbate," admits an interviewee who is now single but was in a long-term relationship until his partner died. "I think everybody does, and right now that is my main outlet." When with someone else, he says he likes to "kiss, fondle, touch, and caress." Certain sexual practices are turnoffs, though. "I don't like anal sex at all and prefer a partner that does not like or require it." He feels wearing condoms is a necessary, if limiting, precaution. "They sort of minimize the physical sensation, but you have to use a little common sense today."

A few of the men have stopped seeking out sexual partners. "I'm not actively sexual now. My primary stimulation is [watching] videos," says one of the single men. "Mutual oral sex" was usually what he engaged in when he still had partners. "I never cared for receptive anal sex, although I've been the active partner," he adds. "Fortunately, not being anal receptive is probably why I'm still alive at this age."

Another man who is now in a relationship exclusively engages in oral sex, both actively and passively. He confesses he doesn't wear condoms. "I haven't been doing it. However, I've had very few sex partners, and besides, I don't like condoms." He doesn't have difficulty getting or maintaining an erection but reports, "Right now I'm having problems with ejaculation—something called reverse ejaculation—and it's related to the medication I'm taking. Just before ejaculation you don't get the real high thing, and then when you go, there's nothing." He hopes he will be medication-free in the future and that his sexual functioning will return to normal.

One man who has experienced erectile dysfunction thought the problem was psychological at first, but his doctor explained that it was "strictly a physical thing that had gone wrong in my body—nothing to do with my head." He says his doctor also told him, "'Think of the penis as a bathtub. What is missing in the bathtub is water. What is missing in the penis is blood.' We tried different ways to deal with the issue. The solution for me is a pump device that drives blood to the penis."

RECREATIONAL SEX

"If it's understood between the partners, I don't have a problem with it, as long as they handle it in a responsible way and take care of themselves."
—*Warde Laidman*

One of the most striking differences between gay and straight relationships is how sex outside the relationship is handled. The 41 men interviewed have differing views on recreational sex. For most of the men, it boils down to whatever works best for a particular individual or couple.

Mel Clark engages in recreational sex, yet he has had two long-term relationships. His heterosexual marriage lasted for nearly 17 years, and he has been in a relationship with a man for an equal period of time. "I see no difference between a straight marriage and a gay marriage," Mel says. "When I was in the straight marriage, I played around with guys, and now I still play around with guys if I'm out of town, or [my partner is] out of town." Mel adds, "Normally, we don't talk about it. If an encounter was unusually good or interesting, we'll usually say something about it later. It's not anything we hide from each other, but we don't flaunt it either." Mel and his partner occasionally engage in three-way sex. "A few years ago, the doorbell rang one night at home. I answered the door, and this guy I didn't know said, 'Oh, you're not the right one.' I replied, 'Well, come on in,' and I took him upstairs. He saw my partner and said, 'Yeah, that's him,' and he ended up carrying on with us. It seemed he had followed my other half home one night when I was out of town." For Mel, recreational sex is usually a once-every-two-weeks event, frequently at an adult movie theater. "I tried meeting some people online. I met three men, and there's one that I see occasionally." He says he goes to the baths "when I'm out of town," but he doesn't like bars. "They bore me to death."

According to George Casper, "Getting pleasure from sex is normal and natural, part of the way we were created, and that's good." He adds, "If recreational sex works for partners, that's just fine if there isn't deception. I believe deception breaks down relationships." George recalls one relationship where his partner wanted them to be monogamous. "I found it easy to agree and stick to that." But in other relationships where fidelity wasn't mutually agreed upon from the start, George has had sex with other men. He thinks that part of the reason why a recent relationship ended was because he was engaging in recreational sex. "My partner was upset about that. I don't think there was a double standard, but emotionally it affected him much more deeply than it did me.... My partner didn't expect my outside sex to affect him the way it did, but it did, and that became a problem." The lesson George draws from the experience is that partners should establish early on "mutually agreeable" rules about recreational sex.

Bud Jordan believes recreational sex may have helped his relationship with Vic. "[It] certainly didn't hurt it. One reason we stayed together the way we did—and not just the first years but later down the line—is because we both agreed that something new might not hurt as long as when it was over, it was over." Still, recreational sex was not one of Bud's favorite activities. "Vic liked it. I'm not saying I didn't like it, but he liked it a hell of a lot more than I did. He liked younger; I was always for older." Sometimes they had group sex and shared sexual partners. "We had parties where, before the night was over, the bedrooms were full of people. We traveled in the car a lot, and Vic picked up hitchhikers once in a while and he'd bring them home, but that would be it." Bud admits to some discord because of one man he saw outside the relationship, though. "There was a period when I got carried away. I saw this guy too often, and I shouldn't have. It was causing friction. It didn't last."

Recreational sex is "fine" for both Bill Strong and his long-term partner. "Perhaps everyone should do it," says Bill. "In my case it works very well, but at the same time I am 100% satisfied with my partner, so I do not go out looking for sex. The only rule we have is [to practice] safe sex and wear a condom." For Bill and his partner, recreational sex includes engaging in three-ways together with another man as well as individually having sex with other men. Bill says they meet sex partners through "a nudist group we belong to and at other functions…of that nature."

Ben Fowler is six months into a relationship with his younger partner, Lee, whom he sometimes refers to as 'Boy.' Ben expresses a somewhat relaxed attitude toward recreational sex. "It can be risky and damaging, but if anyone thinks they're going to get into a monogamous relationship for the rest of their lives, that's not always going to happen because men are sexual beings. As Helen Gurley Brown said, 'If men don't get it at home, they're going to get it someplace.' Men need an outlet—often. Just check the tearooms, the tubs, and the parks." Nevertheless, Ben's relationship with Lee has been monogamous so far. "I have not had any outside sex other than on the Internet." Ben's cybersex contacts include men who visit his full-leather Web site, Daddy Ben's, which he calls "a big ego trip for me and [is] seen all over the world." Daddy Ben's attracts quite a few younger Net surfers. "Lots of visitors are 30-year-olds. It blows my mind—what they see in an old daddy who is 77. A 25-year-old from Spain told me, 'You are the hottest man I've ever seen on the Net.' It's an ego booster—keeps me young." When asked about having in-person sexual encounters with his site's visitors, Ben says he would have to discuss the possibility with Lee first. For his part, Lee acknowledges, "Given the fact [that] I like giving up some control for the daddy/boy aspect of the relationship, if Daddy Ben wants to do that, I would not have a problem with it, though I would be very nervous having other people around. It would depend on what [kind of] sex [and to] what degree—cuddling, oral sex, anal sex. We'll have to look at it. We haven't had that situation arise as yet." As to whether Lee may engage in recreational sex, Ben insists, "Boy will be strictly monogamous," but then poses an intriguing question: "If he participates in sex with another and me, is that being monogamous? I don't know."

Robert Bettinger states, "Recreational sex has to be up to each individual. I don't pass judgment on what other people do; I just make my own decisions." His experience with recreational sex has varied with what relationship he has been in. "I've had relationships that were not exactly open, with both parties [having recreational sex], but when I discovered my partner was having recreational sex, I engaged in it. I would not do that on my own." Regarding one relationship, he notes, "Sex outside [the relationship] was just plain fun, nothing more—a pleasant and good experience." In his present relationship there has been no recreational sex. "I'd love to, but my partner would not be comfortable with it."

Fred and Clee think recreational sex is OK, but Clee says, "Our main emphasis was always coming home to be together." In earlier years, "when the baths were open, we went—when you didn't have to be afraid [of contracting HIV]. But now, it's just altogether different. I wouldn't touch one." Fred says that sex outside their relationship never got to the point of threatening them as a couple. If either man saw a potential threat developing, he ended the contact. But they never had set rules for sex outside their relationship, "I guess it was more of a feeling," Clee acknowledges, "than a face-to-face talk and agreement."

Ed Conlon views recreational sex as up to the individual and acknowledges that partners "may be committed to one another but have needs." Occasionally, he and his lover, Shawne, have sought out recreational sex by mutual consent. "I was his [Shawne's] first lover," explains Ed. "He did not grow up in a gay environment, and

I wanted him to experience it. When I felt secure, I encouraged him to have sex with somebody else so he wouldn't feel cloistered. I took him to a bathhouse, and he did not appreciate that. However, the night we were there, I did. It was a release for me." Ed believes both partners in a relationship must reach an agreement about recreational sex and should be open about discussing it with each other. Ed advises new couples: "Do not start off with [recreational] sex, because it takes a long time to fall in love. Recreational sex should wait until love is secure."

Norm Self sees himself on the edge of a relationship, "one of only two that I've ever taken as serious prospects." Norm feels it is an error to think that "fidelity equals monogamy. I think that fidelity has to do with mutual trust." Partnership, he says, is "a connection that is unique. To say that I can only have sex with my 'married' partner expresses a fear that a sexual encounter with somebody else will turn my affections there, that I'll go away and love that person." He adds, "If I were connected with somebody who's that ambivalent or that shallow about his commitment, I would have a bigger problem than where he has his sex." Norm then asks, "What does it mean to be connected and to be really faithful to one another? I've had sex with countless men. I cannot imagine ever having accomplished the repertoire of sexual experience and joy with any one person, no matter how inventive the two of us may be. My partner benefits from those experiences I've had outside this relationship and I benefit from the relationships he's had." Norm concedes, though, "I would be willing, if things otherwise were really grooving, to negotiate monogamy, at least on a trial basis: 'Let's try this for six months, if it isn't working for me, I'll let you know. I will not violate the agreement without telling you first.' The issue, then, becomes a matter of integrity."

Charles says that recreational sex was never an issue in his relationship. He and his partner engaged in it "occasionally," but he feels it was "not a habit-forming thing. The rule was we do not own each other. You love somebody; you do not own them."

Frank Poe says of recreational sex, "I think it's all right for the person that wants to do it, but at my age I'm not too interested, though I was at one time." He and his partner, Ed, engaged in very little recreational sex while they were together. "Maybe twice, and Ed was involved too. I didn't enjoy it too much, but Ed liked it." As far as Frank knows, Ed didn't have any other recreational sex contacts outside their relationship.

Not all of the men, however, are accepting of sex outside a committed relationship, Milton Lestz for one. "If you have a partner you're in love with, you have sex with that partner—and that partner only. If you're single, then you have no responsibilities; you can do whatever you want." The survivor of a 35-year relationship that ended with his partner's death several years ago, Milton states, "We lived like a married couple. There was [no recreational sex] for either party."

Robert Tingling doesn't believe in recreational sex for men in committed relationships, either, "especially with the sort of diseases around." When asked about the relationships he's been in, he avers, "We never had any recreational sex." Bill Worrall similarly disapproves of recreational sex. "I'm old-fashioned. I want a monogamous relationship, where both are faithful to each other." Robert of Palm Desert simply dismisses the notion of recreational sex: "I don't approve of it."

Jim of Michigan is no less critical of sex outside a relationship. "I don't like it," he says. "If you say you're going to be monogamous, be that." He feels that recreational sex ended his relationship. "I'd always thought, just like in the straight world, [we'd be] sitting together on the porch in that rocking chair, but it didn't work that way." He suspects his partner had engaged in sex outside their relationship "from day one. It was going on probably 50% of the time."

Lee Denman says he has "a hard time understanding" why either partner in a gay relationship would engage in recreational sex. He asks, "When you care about somebody, why do you need somebody else for a few seconds of climax? Recreational sex is more like a drug to me than something necessary to life [and] doesn't lend itself to a long-term relationship."

Ed of Oakland and his partner, Bob, have been monogamous over the course of their 55-year relationship. Ed is troubled by the experience of a gay relative who lives in Seattle. "[The relative] is about 47 and living in an open relationship. When he told us about his open relationship, neither Bob nor I really understood what 'open relationship' meant. The thought of it is difficult for us to accept, but it's there, and that's another generation. For my generation, it was us—the two of us, that is, like my parents."

Norman Eckelberger swears he was completely monogamous during his 27-year relationship with a man 14 years his senior. "I have never been a promiscuous-type person—never. In fact, the 27-year relationship ended because he died of cancer. I cannot speak completely for him, but I can say this: I did absolutely nothing else. It was completely monogamous." Norman says that his partner's death 10 years ago "threw me for a loop—it really did." He acknowledges that recreational sex "is out there," but he doesn't believe in engaging in it. His current relationship with Steve Scott is monogamous. Steve describes recreational sex as "deadly," though he admits that before AIDS he was "promiscuous as hell."

José Sarría observes, "I've always said, 'What the other one doesn't know isn't going to kill them,' but I don't encourage promiscuity." José counts "four great loves" in his life, but now "they're all dead." He insists there was no recreational sex in any of his relationships. "No, no, no, we were very true to one another."

Bill Worrall says he "was probably 99% faithful" to his now-deceased partner. He thought his partner was too, "but after he passed away I found out how much he had been playing around." Bill believes his partner contracted HIV through recreational sex. "I traveled, doing concerts for a music company. That was his opportunity to go back into the leather bars of Hollywood, where he was when I met him." Bill recalls that when he returned from one music tour his partner told him, "I tested positive, so we can't have sex anymore." Bill adds, "We lived [together] two years afterward, sleeping in the same bed but not having any sex because he wanted to protect me."

Frank Poe has also had a bad experience with recreational sex. He still vividly remembers that one night almost 20 years ago, when he and his partner used to go to bars together. "Two men came on to us. They wanted to come to our house—insisted, really. They followed us in their car to our house, came in the house, pulled a gun on us, hit my partner on the head with the gun, tied us up, separated us, and took everything they could put in their car. I don't think they were gay men. [They were] just interested in our money and whatever else they could get. After they left, I got untied pretty quickly and ran to the bedroom where my partner was tied up. He was moaning and groaning, needed help. I called a friend who said, 'You better get him to the hospital.' Thinking my partner wouldn't want to go to the hospital, I had a doctor over instead who treated him." Neither man reported the robbery and assault to the local police because of the antigay climate of the times. "I didn't want the police questioning me about how I knew these men and all that stuff. We were both acting stupid." As a result of this experience, going to bars for casual sex came to a halt for both Frank and his partner.

Cyprian Fary says of recreational sex, "I don't think I approve. I would like to have just one friend." He acknowledges, though, that in the past he has had sex outside his relationships, and so have his partners. He doesn't see "that I was involved in it," though. For now, he says, he would "just rather...see what the situation is."

John Kiley's views about recreational sex have changed over time. "When I was younger I couldn't understand it. Either you were together or you weren't. As I've grown older, I've become more accepting of people who have others in their lives. Whatever works, works. Gene and I don't have recreational sex outside of our own relationship, but I'm more accepting of it now."

Jon Borset thinks recreational sex is OK "as long as both parties agree" but also notes, "If I was in a relationship, I wouldn't want it to be open."

Jon's good friend Tom Pait says, "If you're going to be a dedicated couple, then I don't think you should be fooling around." He admits, though, to a double standard in his own relationships. "I was very bad: I could do it, but they couldn't. I'd go out and cruise, pick up somebody and carry on with him. It was just something I couldn't control." Yet if his partner ever "looked cross-eyed at somebody," he'd have a fit.

CHAPTER 9

Spirituality, Ethics, and Death

BELIEF IN A SUPREME BEING

"My sexuality is a gift from the creator."
—*Rod Harrington*

A recent poll by *The New York Times* reported that between 92% and 97% of the American population believe in God, 80% believe in some form of afterlife, and 70% believe in hell. In the same poll it was found that 60% of Americans go to church once a month or more—that number has been constant for 40 years—and 75% believe in miracles. Only 3.2% of Americans say they don't believe in God. Eleven percent of the population, however, are not affiliated with any specific religious denomination—a number that has doubled since the early 1970s.

The 41 men interviewed for this book tell a somewhat different story. As with the *Times* survey, the majority say they believe in a supreme being, though several harbor doubts about an afterlife. The major difference in respect to the findings of the *New York*

Times poll is that a significant number of the men interviewed believe in neither a supreme being nor an afterlife. Interestingly, two of the men, Robert Bettinger and Norm Self, both ordained clergy, state that their beliefs have shifted from the religious orthodoxy of their training to something beyond that.

"The doctrine and discipline of the Episcopal Church was pretty much all of my career," says Robert Bettinger, but his religious stance has since become radically less doctrinal. "I went from being an Episcopal priest to being an ecumenical chaplain to being a person of multi-religious practices." Concerning his beliefs now, he states, "I don't know if I believe in an afterlife or in reincarnation, but I do believe the most important thing for me right now is to focus on this life and let the other life take care of itself." Robert maintains his membership in the Episcopal Church and receives a pension from it but adds, "I also am ordained in a New Age religion. I'm not focused on one religion; I endorse and embrace a lot of spiritual teachings: Native American, New Age, Buddhist." Summing up, he says, "I believe in creation, but I believe there are different views on creation and on a supreme being, and that all of them have something to offer."

An ordained United Methodist minister, Norm Self reflects on how his spiritual outlook has evolved: "All I can say is that there is something bigger than I am. There's something bigger than the sum total of all of us together. Most efforts to speculate about what that is or to give it a name are misbegotten." In recognition of his "love/hate relationship with religion and theology," he adds, "I believe that life goes on, that I'll be part of it, but I don't have any notion of how."

John Peters is certain that a supreme being exists. "Definitely," he avers. And when asked if he believes in the afterlife he replies,

"I sure do." Ed Conlon, a baptized Catholic (although his mother was Protestant) is also a believer. "I absolutely believe in and adore Christ. I cannot see a crucifixion representation in a movie or somewhere else without becoming very emotional."

In contrast, Lee Denman considers belief in a supreme being and an afterlife "difficult, unless you want to believe in one of the greatest practical jokes that ever existed." He sees a possibility of further existence but remains skeptical about "what most people define as an afterlife."

ORGANIZED RELIGION

"Religions are one of the worst things that ever happened to the world."

—*Jon Borset*

Christianity, and in fact most other major religions, have historically been extremely homophobic, and this legacy has a direct effect on the religious affiliation of gay men today. Gay men have not only left established religious organizations but have formed gay-friendly churches and synagogues. Most notable among these is the Metropolitan Community Church (MCC), a gay- and lesbian-friendly Christian church that now numbers over 42,000 members in 16 countries.

In contrast, the Southern Baptist church is among the most notoriously homophobic denominations. Bud Jordan says, "My whole family is devoutly Southern Baptist. My great-grandfather was a minister in the church and built the local church. His daughter, my grandmother—all of them—were far-right Baptists.

To this day I cannot stand the Baptists. They just hate us, despise us, and are trying to get rid of the gays. I can't stand them anymore and [have] forsaken my religion." Bud no longer attends church and does not see religion as important in his life.

The Roman Catholic church has also been notoriously homophobic. John Schiappi, raised as a Roman Catholic, is now an Episcopalian. "In college I was the typical fallen Catholic. I became agnostic verging on atheist, and I maintained this for years. When I got into AA—and although AA makes a real effort saying you can define 'Higher Power' however you want—that experience played into the spiritual dimensions in my life, and I ended up joining the Episcopal church, which is as close to Catholicism as I want to go." John says, "Many of my gay friends who were involved in the church have died, so my church involvement is lessening year by year."

Jim Mitchell also belongs to the Episcopal church, which he attends "pretty regularly, not 52 times a year, but at least once or twice a month." Years ago, while attending college, Jim had decided he wanted to be a priest. He "went for counseling on the subject," and was honest with the counselor about being gay. "The counselor told me, 'You won't be allowed in the church.' He actually threw me out of his office."

George Casper had a similar experience. He was a theology student in the early 1950s and on track to becoming a priest when he realized he was gay. "At the beginning of my final year, the dean discovered that I was gay, not that I had done anything about it." The dean told George that he had information from a third party to whom George had confided he was gay. The dean issued George an ultimatum: "[I] could either admit it or submit myself to a trial before the faculty. Well, I said, 'I am homosexual,' so I was out. I was on the street, married, and my wife was pregnant—got no points for that, though."

In San Francisco, Fred belongs to the Methodist Church, while his partner, Clee, is a member of the Church of the Brethren. Clee considers himself a regular communicant to whom religious affiliation is "very important," even though the church he once attended is now closed. Fred describes himself as a "backsliding Methodist" and says that religion is not an important part of his life. Both men remember when they first were a couple and had to attend separate churches because going to church together was not acceptable. "I had to go to one church; Fred had to go to the other," remembers Clee.

Will Belais is a devout member of the Unitarian Universalist church. "The adjective 'devout' is important," he says, "because I really am. I never miss church." Will describes religious affiliation as "a major part of my life. I need a church community; I need Sunday services; I need to have a place to go to during the week. But I don't use church as a place to take care of my psychological needs. It's a place for my meditative needs."

Cyprian Fary's religious beliefs were formed during his childhood in his native village in Czechoslovakia. "All people in the town that I was born in were Catholic. There was no other religion, only Roman Catholic." Cyprian adds rather bluntly, "The priests did nothing right. There were so many poor people, and the priests had big stomachs and were asking always for money, money, money, money."

Ordained United Methodist minister Norm Self declares, "Religion is diabolical in its treatment of homosexuality, [but] I don't want to be too hard on religion, because the only way religion can exist is in the hearts and minds of people, and people generally have been diabolical toward gay people. But religion is one weapon that misinformed and ignorant people use." Norm says he sees "some courageous souls, some gay and some not, a few beacons who have been in the vanguard of breakthrough for the acceptance and celebration of gay and lesbian people." When he looks at religion today, Norm perceives a "conservative Christian mentality backward-looking to a golden age of belief that causes people to reinvent all the old biases, fears, and prejudices, and from there turn sexuality into a moral question, one that says human beings are made to keep rules imposed on them by their religions." Norm feels more comfortable asking two all-important questions: "What did God create here?" and "What are the special gifts of [being] gay?" He then states, "You can't even look at those questions if you start with the premise that gay itself is wrong." Norm believes that most gay churchgoers would rather be in an inclusive congregation, but he acknowledges that all-gay churches are necessary too. "If a separate church is what it takes to get safety, that's it."

Episcopal priest Robert Bettinger's feelings about gay worship houses are "mixed." He asks, "Why repeat something that's so repressing because the teachings are basically so repressing?" On the other hand, he says, "People who establish gay churches are enabling change within some religions."

Jim Mitchell says, "Within some of the sects that officially denounce homosexuality, like Roman Catholics, you can find a welcoming parish. The Episcopal Church doesn't officially condemn [being] gay, but they don't officially OK it either. There are lots of very open parishes; you just have to find one that is welcoming." However, because Jim makes frequent trips from New York City's northern-most suburbs to Appleton, Wis., to visit his disabled ward, he concedes that finding a mainstream church that is gay-friendly often boils down to geography. "I don't go to the Episcopal church in Wisconsin because there isn't one that's open and welcoming," he admits. He attends MCC whenever he is in Appleton. Based on his own experience, Jim feels there is a "definite place" for gay churches.

Mel Clark isn't a regular churchgoer but remarks, "I enjoy church. We go to MCC, the Metropolitan Community Church, in Washington [D.C.] occasionally. [We attended] more often when we lived in Washington, but now it's a commute, so we don't attend services there as frequently. I'm not a firm believer that there has to be an organized church. We each have a responsibility to find belief ourselves. I don't have to go to church to commune with God."

Ron Dropkin sees "a great deal of hypocrisy in organized religion." Gay churches, he thinks, are "a good idea. I'm old enough and wise enough to know some people have a spiritual part of them and a need for organized religion. I know that they've been rejected in their churches and now have gay organizations." Pointing to a nearby gay synagogue, he says, "I know people who have a need to go there. It's wonderful they have it." Ron considers the French philosopher Jean-Paul Sartre "very close" to his own worldview. He states, "This life, to paraphrase Sartre, is a bottomless black abyss and any good that comes out of it is a result of individual action. Good has nothing to do with praying to Jesus or praying to Moses or anyone or anything else. Good has to do with you and your ability to make something of what is nothing."

Jim Edmonds' upbringing was in the Methodist Church, and he has been "grappling" with his church's position on gays. While he cites official opposition to ordaining openly gay ministers in the Methodist church, he sees some "reconciling churches that are very open." His local minister, he believes, would adhere to the majority church opinion in opposition to gays. Yet he and his three sisters are regular communicants as "the only blacks in attendance." At one time Jim attended a gay church, but says, "I really feel that we have to fit into society. In a sense, if we have our own church, we're sort of segregating ourselves."

John Schiappi does not care for how "one-dimensional" gay churches strike him. "To each their own—that's fine. I struggle with not wanting to live my life in a gay ghetto. It's important for me to keep a diversity of friendships, relationships, and activities so that my life isn't completely gay-centric. If I were going to be active in a church, I would want a church that was not one-dimensional."

Ed of Oakland echoes John Schiappi and calls gay churches a "ghetto." He asks, "Why aren't we included in the Temple Emmanuel? Why do we have to have our own Metropolitan Community Church?" He admires the MCC movement but contends that, if he were an Episcopal priest, he "would be embarrassed" that MCC has to exist.

John Peters, a Catholic for whom religion is "very important," feels his church "has not done enough to cater to or minister to homosexuals," although he remains a regular churchgoer. "But they're gradually coming around," he notes. "We have to have more openness. A big obstacle was Cardinal John O'Connor; the Lord took him out of the way." Homophobia in religion "is awful," John adds. "It's not at all Christian to look down on another person, regardless of what they like sexually." He has also worshiped with MCC congregations in Davenport, Iowa, and in San Diego and thinks churches for gay people "are wonderful," but he doesn't like being "segregated."

From his vantage point in Sewanee, Tenn., in "the heart of the Bible Belt," Bill Strong also sees a need for gay churches, if only for the time being. "Gay worship houses are fine. If that's what people need, fine—create their own and go to them." But he thinks the need for such churches "will decline with more acceptance."

ETHICAL PRINCIPLES

"I consider myself a very ethical person. I have a very strong sense of ethics, right and wrong. I've never done anything intentionally that you could call mean or vindictive."

—Ron Dropkin

Whether an individual adheres to a specific religious practice or not, he generally has a set of ethical principles by which he lives his life. The 41 men interviewed are no exception. In fact, most of the men have a strong grasp of the role of ethics in their lives. Not surprisingly, some identify their religious beliefs as forming their moral foundation. Others might be called "postreligious."

A large number of the men adhere to the Golden Rule: "Do unto others as you would have them do unto you." When asked about his personal ethics, Jim Edmonds responds, "I think it's pretty much the Golden Rule." Bill Worrall agrees. "I was taught the Golden Rule by my father. I try to treat people well, never do anything to harm people." Fred also looks to the adage for guidance. "Generally speaking, I'd say [I live by] the Golden Rule. If you do goodness, some goodness comes back to you."

John Schiappi states, "A major facet of my life is wanting to reach out and help other people, not hurt other people." Likewise, Charles says, "My mother brought me up to believe that you don't hurt anybody." John Kiley vows, "I don't want to hurt anyone or to lie. I just want to be what I think of as a good person." Milton Lestz tries to go out of his way to help people. "A principle of mine is to help others," he says. "Helping people" is also of prime importance to Bud Jordan, who says, "If you want to do something good, do it for a person. Be kind; do what you can for humanity." Richard Malloy comments on the value of good works: "Mostly it's kindness. Only what you give away is really yours. I've learned an awful lot about this in my hospice work with the dying." Norman Eckelberger sums up, "I try to be as honest and as good as I possibly can. I'm not saying that I'm perfect. I stray, but I try not to stay strayed."

For John Peters, religion and ethics converge. "Yes, I believe in God, and I still feel He has control." Rod Harrington sounds a similar note. "My ethics and spirituality have been formed through Christianity. That's what I was raised in." Bill Strong says his Catholic background "enters into it: belief in a supreme being. But at the same time, I do a lot of things that Catholics don't believe in."

Robert Bettinger characterizes his ethics as "postreligious." He adds, "I have basic practices of human concern and concern for the universe. When I support the Sierra Club, for instance, I support the universe and human rights. In supporting other conservation issues, human rights, and earth rights, I focus on the total universe."

Norm Self states, "I consider myself an exceptionally passionately ethical person, but I have great suspicion of codes." He continues, "We try to get people into faith by making them moral beings. That's the upside-down, bass-ackwards way. If we can contact the spirit of human beings and enliven that spirit, if we can create spiritual beings, the morality will flow out of a spiritual commitment." Concerning the ethics of sexuality he comments, "We typically see sex as the test case of morality. The question boils down to this: Is life being served by this sexual encounter, or am I deluding myself because I want gratification, and I'll do whatever it takes to get it? Buying, stealing, conniving, deceiving, getting the gratification any way I can, that's immoral. When I engage in an encounter that ultimately becomes sexual, I'm engaged as a whole person. There are some people I don't have sex with because that doesn't [happen]. But when all the ingredients come together, it's something to celebrate."

Lee Denman's exposure to a kaleidoscope of cultures while living abroad has informed his ethical perspective. "Most of the rest of the world is far ahead of the United States in learning that people are people and are getting rid of their prejudices, most of which seem to be generated by religion. The countries that seem to be the most favorable and accepting of all kinds of people, of all races, and anything else seem to be those that have pushed the churches farthest to the side."

Ron Dropkin says, "Although I have no use for organized religion—nor does my mate, and that's one of the reasons we get along so well—I have a very strong sense of ethics, right and wrong. I consider myself a very ethical person." Will Belais expresses a like sentiment, "My ethic is that I must honor the other person—well beyond the idea that one does not steal or murder. Even though I get very angry about religious fundamentalists, I still have to honor them."

DEATH

"When it's time to go, I'm not afraid of it."

—*Jon Borset*

Death, of course, is inevitable. The 41 men express a variety of opinions on what death is and how prepared (or unprepared) they are for it. Most, however, accept that it will come when it comes and seem to find peace in that acceptance.

George of New York City views death as, "the last great adventure. I think you welcome death, and you do go gladly into that good night, because it is a good night, because it is inevitable, and when it comes, you've been at the party a good long time."

Mel Clark says, "I look at death [as being] like when you cut your fingernails. You don't worry about what you cut off; you just throw it away. I think it will be like that when I die. My spirit will go on, but my body will be disposed of. My ashes are to be scattered near Pecos Wilderness in New Mexico and on a beach in New Jersey and wherever else my partner wants to scatter them." While attending a family reunion in Missouri, Mel visited his ancestral burial plot in the local cemetery. "The younger generation—my kids, cousins—were there and enjoyed so much going around looking at the tombstones and seeing who their relatives were. I thought, even though my ashes will be scattered, I probably should have a tombstone in that cemetery."

Others seem to be not as prepared. According to Richard Malloy, life for him and his partner Tucker "has been a wonderful, superglorious party. There were times when we ran out of money, when we wished people would get the hell out of our way. But it's been a beautiful party, and as in every party, somebody has to leave first. Then there's one left to clean up the mess."

Death doesn't worry Jim Edmonds. "I've had heart surgery. Having gone through that experience some 17 years ago and survived, I realize that it's the present—the time I have now—that's important, and I try not to be too concerned about dying."

Lee Denman says, "I try to live for today. I went through a period a year ago when I was told that I could drop dead anytime. I proved the doctors wrong and have since recovered. My great-grandfather lived to be 96, and he was still farming behind a mule with a hand plow. My family has been fairly long-lived. I wouldn't mind seeing 100, but not from a nursing home."

John Kiley also does not want to live beyond good health. "I would be very unhappy [if I were ever] sick or incapacitated." Steve Scott agrees. "I believe in suicide [in cases of incapacitation or terminal illness]. I think I would just as soon do myself in, if I had go to a nursing home." He quips, "Living a long life? Absolutely not unless my health held up."

Other men express exactly the opposite sentiment. Norm Self has "already made preparations" in the event he'd ever need extended nursing care. "I'm ready," he says. "I'm not eager for it, but preparation has been a part of what's made my life so joyous— letting go of wanting to acquire, to achieve, and allowing myself to be into what is now. I expect that today is going to be delicious, that tomorrow is going to be better. I live each day in that spirit. Now, if I start to fail and can't get around, then my take would be to find a habitat where I can be infirm and still be engaged."

Ed of Oakland looks at death from the perspective of a long-time resident of a lifetime-care facility. "Here we face death all the time.... I may die in this apartment, which I hope I do. If I have to be cared for through nursing care, then I could still live in this apartment independently to a degree. Or I could be in our assisted living area, where people have more help. Now, we go to breakfast, lunch, and dinner in the dining room. But if I need medical care around the clock, it's there."

Will Belais is not overly concerned with death. "I don't think much about it, really." He says, "I read a book some time ago called *Dare to Be 100*. I liked the book's simple advice: First, never give in to frailty if you can help it. That's what I've been working on: Do not give in to frailty. The book's second piece of advice is to keep active as much as possible. That's why I sing and play the piano, why I do all the things I do."

Robert Bettinger says he is content to live out the rest of his life "and not worry about dying...about when things change in my body or my opportunities lessen. Just adjust to it as best I can and stay a happy person as long as I can."

A few of the men still struggle with their mortality, though. "Death is a frequently recurring thought," Warde Laidman confides. "The whole aging process is not easy for me. I have some work to do in the whole field of aging."

John Schiappi underwent surgery for prostate cancer in 1995 and says that since then "the PSA levels have begun edging up gradually, indicating the cancer was not fully captured by the operation." He is not discouraged, though, and adds, "In a way, that's almost good for me, because I know now that I am not going to have to worry about living to be age 90. Having grown up as a Depression baby in a family that didn't have much money, I've had this nagging concern about [whether I will] have enough money. Now I know for sure I will have enough money. I worry about

Alzheimer's and senility, about losing the quality of life. Being a highly sexual man with prostate cancer, I worry about losing the sexual function."

Ed Conlon has also made peace with death while undergoing cancer treatment. He says, "I am quite prepared to face death. I have made peace with myself. I've had such a wonderful life that I cannot be selfish and deny death. I mean that sincerely."

There's still one thing George Casper admits he doesn't like about death, though. "The idea of death is I'm not going to know how this, that, or the other thing turned out." But not knowing doesn't cause him much anxiety. "In some respects, I look forward to death, particularly if it's easy."

CHAPTER 10

The Future

GROWING OLDER

"My body has aged in years. But me, the person, the individual inside the body, I don't think is any older today than when I was 25."

—*Lee Denman*

Most of the men have found growing older to be a positive experience. Some are ambivalent about the process, mainly due to health concerns, and just a few find it an unwelcome experience.

Jim Mitchell doesn't fear aging. "I never feared growing old, and I still don't. Sometimes I fear for my health. I'm concerned about that now, and I'm changing some things about my life, but I don't fear or worry about growing old."

Norm Self says, "I like being over 65. I like being retired. I like being as old as I am, and I like the prospect of getting older. But I don't feel old." It comes as a surprise to Norm to look at his contemporaries and "see them looking like old people! I'm very blessed to live a lot of my life with young people and have all that exuberance of youth around me all the time." Drawing on an Old Testament metaphor, he says, "I can sit at the city gate and dispense my wisdom. There are a lot of people seeking my wisdom. I say that not arrogantly but with glorious pride and joy, a joy that people want to be with me. I like that. It's part of the gift of being old."

Ed Conlon thinks of aging as "very rewarding, a good experience, one that I appreciate. Besides," he adds, "what's the alternative? No male member of my family has lived beyond 60, and I have reached 72. My grandmother died at 72, and I always thought I would too until I reached her age. Now I know I'm going to break that barrier. I will continue on as long as I can. As long as the quality is there, I want to grow older. I'm very grateful for every day and every year." Ed doesn't even believe he thinks like an old person—as if anyone ever does. "Mentally, I feel you always think younger. I know I do. I don't think 72, I think 42—and that makes me 30 years younger than I am. My body can still move. I'm agile. I can still have sex. Age is on the calendar; it's there. You're not going to change it, but you don't have to become aged."

Robert Bettinger says, "I'm growing older with what I consider to be grace and joy." He cites "good genes and good health" as crucial in his aging process. "I've exercised wisdom to maintain good health. [I've always eaten] good food. I didn't get caught up in excesses and abuses like excessive alcohol. I never used recreational or hard drugs and always took care of my body." Looking ahead, Robert predicts, "I'll continue to do all I can. When my body can't take it anymore, I'll adjust to what has to happen."

John Schiappi says, "I tell people jokingly that the best years of my life have been since age 50. By then you've probably gone about as far in your career as you're going to go, so some of that struggle eases. If you have children, they're grown and on their own.

It's a time to fully enjoy life. For me, a lot of that continued through my 60s." In his 70s, though, John "began to see signs of worrisome health problems." He recalls when he and two friends from London were planning a trip to Nepal. "They both had just turned 50, and I'm wondering, *Am I up to hiking and trekking with them to the extent that they might want to?* Such limitations, inevitably, are going to increase rather than wane, and they're considerations."

For Mel Clark, age is self-perception. "I don't consider myself old, and I don't feel old." He frequently finds himself sizing up a new acquaintance as an "old man," only to later be proved wrong. "I find out he is younger than I am. So a lot of it is your attitude."

Norman Eckelberger views aging as "very interesting, because the older I get, the more I've seen and the more I've progressed." The only thing so far about aging that Norman doesn't like is "getting love handles and more of a stomach on me. Otherwise, it doesn't really bother me."

Jim Edmonds says he doesn't feel old. "I'm enjoying life too much, but I know I'm slowing down." He recognizes the importance of his good health for engaging in the things he likes to do. "As long as I can still get around, I don't think aging is going to bother me," he says, "but I realize that someday I'm not going to be able to do the things that I'm doing now, like play the piano."

The aging experience has been "great" for Dave, but he wishes younger men would "lighten up" in their attitudes toward older gay men. "Look to others and maybe learn something," he instructs. Ron Dropkin and his younger partner, a Japanese man who has become a clothing designer, would certainly agree with Dave. Ron says about younger partner, "When he first came to the United States, he was just starting his career. I've seen him go from nowhere to a high-level job and grow from a child, really, into a man. I think

I have been influential in his social development." Ron says he has "no problem with having grown older."

Bill Worrall says aging is "A-OK" with him. "I'm getting more sexual opportunities than I ever did when I was young. Maybe I'm getting better-looking. Aging is a real plus for me. I feel accepted and wanted. When somebody 40 years younger is attracted to you, it's a real turn-on." Similarly, Ben Fowler says that while aging has been "scary and trying," he's enjoying his sexuality. "Right now, due to my Web site and cybersex, I feel like I'm a hot old leather daddy."

Bill Strong says, "I really don't think of myself as being older, except occasionally when I look in the mirror and don't quite recognize the person looking back. I don't feel a lot different than I did 20 years ago."

Rod Harrington sees himself as having been "in age denial" but thinks he is "now coming out of it. I've been in denial until the last year or two. I've had some back problems and skeletal problems. In the last year or two I haven't liked aging." After divorcing and coming out when he was nearly 50, Rod had thought, *Well, you're going to be an incredibly sorry, pitiful old man.* Instead, he has been pleasantly surprised to have "an incredible circle of friends, many of them younger." A lesson of aging, Rod believes, is to "reach out to people without expectation. If you can reach out to people without expectations, their reaction will astound you."

For Milton Lestz, aging is a mixed bag. "I don't like the lessening of energy that I have…taking a nap every day—I never did that before." On a more positive note, he observes, "I have more time to myself than ever before, more balance in my life. I'm more mature, and I feel emotionally healthier than I ever felt before."

A few of the men struggle with aging. "I don't like it," says

Will Belais. "I'm not aging gracefully. I resist it as much as possible. When people tell me that I'm old, I can't understand what they're saying. My ex-wife tells me that I'm an old man. When I look in the mirror, I get very disappointed. I don't like the look of this tired, wrinkled face. I don't like the aches and pains I have in my joints, but I ignore them. I look at young men on the street in our neighborhood here, and I realize they have a future and I don't."

Several men express simple resignation to aging and eventual death. Bud Jordan says, "No one likes growing older. It didn't bother me too bad until I hit 70. Now, I wouldn't care if I passed on. At almost 74 years, I've lived a full life, and I have not regretted one moment." Frank Poe hasn't minding aging "until the last couple of years." He notes, "Because I live alone, I worry that I might die in my sleep and my poor dog would have to die with me, because nobody would come over here and take her."

"I think Bette Davis said it the best," quips José Sarría. "'Growing old is a bitch.' It's not always easy. You have to be able to bend your ideas, your ways of thinking, to quickly change things that you were brought up with."

ADVICE FOR YOUNGER MEN

"Start saving money. Until about 25 years ago, I didn't have a dime in the bank, but I started saving then and now I'm pretty well off."

—*Jon Borset*

Financial planning and security are in the forefront of advice the 41 men interviewed urge on younger men. Other advice deals with relationships, lovers, relating to older men and to society at large, a variety of health issues, and sex.

"The worst thing that can happen to you is getting old and being poor," says Steve Scott. "It's a terrible thing, and I've seen it happen to people I know. Start preparing financially—now!" Bud Jordan says, "Try to be independent, but have a little money when you get older, because you're going to need it." Lee Denman warns, "No matter what type of business you're in, don't think the retirement benefits of the individual company will support you. Make sure you have your own retirement money under your control and that you keep building it. Don't rely on your employer or your own company. Do it for yourself."

Norm Self always counsels his younger friends to plan financially. "Start a plan of putting away financially so that by the time you reach your mid 50s you'll be able to decide if you want to keep on working, how much you want to work, and how you want to live." Though younger people should plan for the future, Norm hastens to add, "The present shouldn't be ignored. I say, 'Don't live in the future, live now.' Don't wait for permission to be who you are. Choose to be who you are now."

George Casper believes that investing money wisely while young is "very important, so as to have a nest egg when you're old." He knows, he says, because "it was difficult for me to do that because I had a wife, children, a divorce, and all those things were very, very costly. But for guys who are single or coupled with a man, they better be looking to their financial future." Unfortunately, George doesn't "see many financial plans" among his younger friends. "I talk to lots of young people and those in early middle age, and so many of them are not preparing for their future."

Robert Bettinger advises, "You will never regret putting money aside for a long-term future. Start financial planning early. Assume that you will live a long time, and that you will live healthy and joyfully." He believes younger men need to make investments.

Ed Conlon also cites the need for wise financial planning and advises, "If you are in love, make sure [that you and your partner] prepare for each other [dying first] and consider each other's future. After all, one or the other may go first."

John Kiley thinks "the best thing" for a younger man to do would be "to find someone to grow old with, and make a plan, set objectives." A successful businessman, John says young people frequently ask him, "What's the secret?" His reply, "What you need to do is figure out what you want and go for it. Write it down; make it real. If your goals aren't real, you'll never achieve them."

Ed of Oakland thinks that young men talk too much about being gay and that what they say is counterproductive to advancing gay and lesbian civil rights. He thinks younger gay men should "keep their mouths shut about being gay and concentrate on being a human being. You earn and learn as you go along. You create change by evolution, not revolution."

Mel Clark emphasizes that younger men need to seek out a life partner and stay committed to him. "I think it's very important to have a partner, especially as you get older. "I wouldn't want to be single and be 85, 90 years old, living alone, and not have anybody to look after me when I need it."

Robert Tingling's advice to younger men is, "Instead of living a ballyhoo life of running here and there, settle down, find somebody you can stay with, and learn to live with people. I don't see gay men learning to live with one another and to share and to compromise. Life is really a compromise, and without it there's nothing doing."

Will Belais says to younger men, "Get out of bars as quickly as possible. Find another place. Nothing important is going to happen in a bar, believe me. Stop playing the sex game; anonymous sex is empty. I've had anonymous sex, and I can tell you it is empty, but it's hard for a young man to understand how empty it really is until he gets a little older. When we're having sex with someone, we should learn to love that person. That's the first thing. The second is find a community for yourself that's inclusive." He condemns the tendency to be "stuck on their youth. It isn't going to last.... Get out of the ghetto of youth. Incorporate right now men of all ages in your lives in meaningful ways—and not as museum pieces. We should father one another. I would like to be the father figure to some of these men, not their 'daddies,' but a father figure, and they can father me. I need them as much as they need me."

Ron Dropkin says, "Find out what your talents are and pursue them. Don't let your dick rule your life. Sex is wonderful, an important part of life, but I know gay people who spent their whole lives getting ready for Saturday night disco. I know other people who spent their lives pursuing a career. They are the ones now ready to retire, successful and established because they pursued a career. I pursued my career, my partner is pursuing his. Spending your life looking in the mirror when you're young thinking, 'Oh, I'm so pretty,' is futile. The most beautiful of us fade physically as we grow older."

Lee Denman places special value on developing a core support network of friends. "You're exceptionally lucky if you have enough good friends in life that you can count them on more than one hand—people you would always help, no matter the problem, people who will help you. People have lots of acquaintances [but] very few friends. Treasure your friends."

In much the same vein, John Schiappi advises, "Maintain as diverse and rich a set of relationships as possible. For example, I compare my straight and gay friends who are my age, and I don't see many gay men my age who are in long-term relationships, but I do see lots of my straight friends in longtime marriages. But in many ways I'm blessed, compared to my straight friends, because I've been forced to seek a diversity of friendships and interests, whereas my married friends are looking at more of a void in their senior years."

Robert Bettinger cautions younger men to lead lives of moderation. "Never do anything to excess, either recreational things or physical things. A spiritual message I got early in my life is 'all things in moderation.' You don't have to worry about what you do if you do it in moderation. Be concerned too about what you do to other human beings, how what you do impacts their life." Younger men, he believes, "need to take better care of their health than a lot of them do. I hope they would not smoke, would not drink excessively, and would leave the more dangerous drugs alone. And remember that AIDS still kills people."

Milton Lestz also warns against the threat of AIDS and other dangers of fast living. "Make sure to use your money wisely and invest so you'll have it when they're older. And don't burn out too soon. Eat and live healthy; get eight hours sleep every night. Don't hang out at bars all the time and be careful with sexuality. Use rubbers."

John Peters sees smoking as a major health issue. "I recommend to anybody who's smoking to quit. Put the money that you spend on those damn cigarettes in the till. I see so many people who are dying of emphysema from smoking—it's a miserable life." John quit smoking in his 30s, in part because of the cost, and saved the money. "I put aside about three quarters that I saved every day."

Charles thinks young men "should not be so cavalier. Many seem to feel that they are God's answer to all of humanity." He adds, "Most young gay people are blatantly rude, sarcastic, unthinking, and careless in their remarks" to older men. Charles suggests that younger gay men "use common sense; realize with every heartbeat that you're older than you were the heartbeat before. Aging comes to all of us. Don't fight it. Age gracefully without being frustrated by it."

Bill Worrall offers similar advice. "I get into an online chat room, then somebody older comes in and all the twinkies put him down. They better wake up and smell the coffee; they're not getting any younger themselves. A lot of them have the Peter Pan syndrome—always 18 and pretty—but it's not going to happen." Young men, Bill thinks, "aren't preparing themselves to be older or associating with older men in most cases."

Jim Edmonds thinks involvement by younger men in organizations that include older people is healthy. "Get involved with organizations that [welcome people of] varied ages," he says. "I'm involved in a group in Seattle that has all ages, and that's very helpful." Tom Pait also suggests that younger men "might try accepting older people in their lives, having older friends."

Ben Fowler states, "Young men need to learn that life is not over at 40. But after 40 you have to make the effort to reach out to people. Learn to handle rejection, be proud of who you are, and love yourself."

Fred says, "Honesty with your partner is number one." He also cites the need for younger men to accept that aging is inevitable and suggests they "maintain social relations with older people and accept them as older." Most younger men, he thinks, are "just too busy with their life to even consider cultivating and knowing older men. But I think once in a while they should stop and just assess the concept in their own minds."

Perhaps summarizing the advice of all the men, José Sarría says, "Live today in a way that will help you tomorrow."

ENVISIONING THE FUTURE

"My life is going to be very exciting. I have lots of things planned, lots I'm going to do, like another trip to Europe. Life is beautiful, even though sometimes it's a pain in the butt. I'm excited about it."

—*José Sarría*

The 41 men interviewed voice many concerns about the future, but overall their outlook is positive. Though there are worries about money and health, many of the men have plans to travel, to enter into a relationship, and to just simply enjoy what life has to offer.

Bill Worrall sees a lover in his future. He states, "I'm really concentrating on a lover. Right now, I have three ads on the Internet and I'm getting a good response. But most of my responses so far have been from around the world, which doesn't do me any good." Bill still feels optimistic about his prospects. "I think it's going to happen. I'm willing to move to be with a partner." A Canadian and a documented U.S. resident, he considers medical coverage a major relocation issue. "If I live in another country or return to Canada, I'll get Social Security sent to me." Health insurance, though, is not so portable, and that's an issue for Bill, even though his health currently is "pretty good."

Milton Lestz wants a man in his life too. "I'm hoping there will be a man in my life, but as hard as I work at it, that doesn't seem to be happening." Like Bill Worrall, he remains optimistic, though. "I don't look ahead. I try to take one day at a time."

Rod Harrington says he is looking forward to retirement within the next few years. "I'm going to retire and fix up an old house. I want to travel. I spent half a day in Florence, Italy; I'd like to spend a month. I love New York City. I want to sublet an apartment and live in New York some winter. I'm seriously thinking of getting a graduate degree." He adds, "I live my life in a way that tells the people who are around me that it's OK to be gay. I make no apologies. I think people, particularly younger ones, really, really want to hear that. And that's why I'm not lonely and have a full social life. I don't have to go to the city or the bars. Life comes to me." Noting his parents' longevity, Rod feels he has many active years left. "My dad lived to 93, my mother to 92. I'm counting on the same. I'm hoping for that."

Several of the men who are city dwellers are thankful for rent control, which has enabled them to continue their standard of living. San Francisco resident Tom Pait says, "If they keep the rent laws like they are right now, I hope to at least stay where I'm living for another five or 10 years." He plans on maintaining his excellent health and level of physical activity as well. "I love race-walking and fast-walking. If I stop running, then I will start fast-walking."

Tom's friend Jon Borset also cites rent control as a reason to remain in his San Francisco apartment, although he also has a place in the Sierras. "I might move to the mountains, but I really prefer the city, and [like] going to the mountains when I want to." When asked if he plans to continue race-walking, Jon says, "I take my cue from Tom. [He's] nearly five years older than me, and he's really in wonderful shape. I think Tom has decided not to run marathons anymore because the training is a bit too much for him, but then I always thought he overtrained. My training [method] is just the minimum, so maybe I can keep going even until 75 and compete in the marathon and race-walk events. I'm in good health now. My mother lived to 96, so maybe I have a few good genes."

Ed Conlon worries about the cost of housing, "I rent, and at 72 I'm not going to buy, and I don't want to have to downgrade." A cancer patient, he says he is "concerned, not worried" about his health. "Worry never helps you. But being concerned can help, so I keep up on cancer cure news. I immediately bring information I see to my doctor and question him about cures." Ed says he and his partner Shawne hope to "enjoy ourselves as much as possible" over the next several years. Ed elaborates, "When I say that, I mean enjoy recreation. If we want, take mini-vacations to Vegas, to Laguna Beach, to bring something new into our lives—the sun, the water, gambling. Do frivolous things, because I think everybody's life should be filled with a little frivolity."

Steve Scott says a move might be in his future. "Most of my friends live in Palm Springs, although I have a lot of friends here [in Palm Desert]. I like the Palm Springs village life and being close to the Palm Canyon area, the main drag—I could walk there." A novelist who publishes his work "for self-fulfillment," Steve expects to continue writing. "I'm financially secure, I have a lot of friends, and I'm very happy writing. It's part of my life. In the next five years, I'm sure I will have another novel, maybe short stories too."

Says Fred: "The next five years of my life will see changes, that's for sure." Clee chimes in, "What they will be, I have no idea, but we must be willing to accept some of them, like health, and look for an answer." Both partners see themselves remaining in their house. Fred says, "If there's illness or sickness, we'll make physical changes in our living quarters to accommodate Clee or myself without having to go to a skilled nursing center." Clee says the ability to adapt is "a must" as people age. "Life is adaptation, and it can be a pleasant experience. That's the way to hit it, because adapting to aging will be easier on you."

Robert Bettinger says his life is good now, and he believes his good health will continue over the next several years. He likes where he lives and what he does. "I have a lot of happiness each day, sing happy songs, take in the beauty of the environment and learn from it. I try to protect the environment but not change it." The ability to hear clearly has been a problem for Robert, but new hearing aids are making his life much better. "I'm relieved of a lot of anxiety from trying to hear in situations where I couldn't. Now I don't have that. I've been [going] years without hearing well, and now I can hear very well. I enjoy being with groups of people, and I no longer feel anxious or withdrawn from the group and conversation." Mindful that his partner is going through a life transition and might relocate, Robert considers what effect that might have: "I would do pretty much the same thing I'm doing: meet new people, keep up with my old friends, continue to enjoy life, and move on. I would feel sad about the separation, but the joy I'm experiencing is where I want to be."

A number of men say they take life just a day at a time, Robert Tingling for one. "As far as I'm concerned, I'm just living from day to day because I don't know what's going to happen." Richard

Malloy says he and his partner Tucker do not engage in "life planning," and deal with life "just the way it is. We live day to day." Cyprian Fary says, referring to the future, "As long as I am healthy, I don't think a thing about it."

Norman Eckelberger also opts for a less rigid approach to the future. "Things in life are undecided; things can happen," he states. "Whatever happens in my life, I'll make the most of it. A friend told me his partner had died and that ended his life too. I feel sorry for him, but you [have to] go beyond that and live…. Life is going to go on. In life you have to be able to roll with the punches, and I expect to."

Bill Strong says, "I'm trying not to have any more heart attacks." But at the same time he wants to travel and do more. He also notes that he and his partner are "going to take some vacations, especially in the winter when my lover, who is in the landscape business, has more time." But he doesn't want to repeat an earlier experience when he owned a condo in Florida. "I was staying there about six months of the year. That was not a good thing for our relationship: being apart."

Ron Dropkin acknowledges, "I do not have the physical stamina today that I had 20, 25 years ago. I have a slight case of arthritis. When I get up in the morning, it takes me a little time to get started. I take a hot shower, a couple of Tylenol or Advil, drink a cup of coffee, and I'm going. And I have the greatest pleasure in going. I don't have to rush, go any place, or do anything. I don't have a job, don't have to be in the office or in school at such and such a time. My mate leaves for work at 9 o'clock in the morning. He's home by 7 o'clock. I have the whole day; nobody's pushing me. If I want to cook dinner, I do, but if I'm not in the mood, I say, 'We're going out for dinner tonight,' or we will order-in Chinese or something. I don't have any pressures. It's wonderful!" Ron adds, "I know now that there are things I cannot control, specifically family. Certain people who upset me, I want out of my life. I do not have to deal with crises or conflict now. I am financially independent, in good health. I have people in my life who give me pleasure and from whom I get pleasure; they are the people I see."

John Schiappi thinks how to handle sex will be the primary issue he'll have to deal with over the next few years. He describes his compulsive sexual activity as a "continuing issue for me, perhaps more of an issue as I get older—being able to handle sex and sexual compulsion in a way that I do not find demeaning to myself. I don't like the image of a dirty old man hanging around the bushes; that's not an appealing image. I want to handle my sexual life in a way that continues the zest without the parts of it that are demeaning to me."

Frank Poe says his goal for the next several years is "to be able to function, to be able to walk and all that. If I get to the point where I need physical help, that's when I should go to an assisted living place."

Ed of Oakland doesn't believe his adjustment to aging over the next several years will be any different from other age passages he has experienced. "I didn't feel I had to adjust at 60, 50, 40, or 30. I have been enjoying people I started with [when I was] 20, and I'm still enjoying them. Some of them have died, but I haven't been that conscious of age. I'm conscious of what's before me at the moment—where I'm living, what I'm doing. I'm 83, and there's nobody on God's earth that's going to change that. I don't worry about it. A lot of my friends are 45, 65, or 80. I want to break down some of these age categories, what I call 'the hardening of the categories,' because that's just a terrible disease."

For Will Belais, part of adapting to aging is adapting to those who are aging with him. "I have to become more accepting of the men who are aging with me. I—and they—are no longer these beautiful guys that you met and knew when you were 25. We just aren't." Part of Will's adapting is behavioral. "I don't go to clubs that cater to young men. That's the first thing I don't do." He notes how something has "happened to us, to the guys I've known for a long time. We've been through the same experiences. If we were to share those experiences with one another, we might find our beauty now is in a different way. That's how to adapt: to find the beauty in a different way."

Norm Self says of his future, "I want to be engaged in telling the good news." He describes the "good news" thus: "That life is wonderful, that gay is a special way of being wonderful. Gay isn't better than straight, but it's certainly as good." He says of his life in general, "I like where I am, but if some compelling vision or some attractive partner lured me to some other place, I could move." Aging, he believes, "gets better if you let it." He adds, "Part of letting aging happen is being vibrantly engaged in what you're doing now, noticing whether it's working, and making adjustments as you go. Plan, and if circumstances knock your plan into a cocked hat, say, 'Oh, I learned something from that,' and alter the plan." Norm concludes, "The way I'm living works for me. Yoga and meditation keep me healthy and feeling younger, but if that changes, I'll adapt."